IN THIS ISSUE

What's Left: Earth's remaining protected wilderness.

LA+ WILD
EDITORIAL

By being *not* human, *not* culture, *not* domestic, *not* artifice, *not* architecture, and *not* garden, the mental geography of 'wild' has been very useful. Wild is everything society defends itself against; and yet, in truth, culture is but a thin film over the surface of evolution's deep pool.

Wild is fundamental. Most creation narratives share the archetype of an emergent order born of, and yet antithetical to, the amorphous miasma that preceded it. The Sumerian god Marduk fought off the tumultuous sea, while the Lord of Judeo-Christianity separated heaven and earth from the void. For the ancient Greeks, Euronyme emerged from Chaos, mated with a serpent, became a dove and then gave birth to Cosmos (order). From Gilgamesh to King Kong–and for all the heroes, saints, and villains in between– wild is simultaneously seductive and threatening. Vanquished or venerated, restrained or released – in both legend and reality the central theme is how we teeter between nature and nurture.

However, two things now make the conceptual organization of wild as 'other' problematic. First, science finds no substantive difference between us and the general 'nature of things'. Second, in its landscape incarnation there just isn't much of the wild stuff left. What remains is a crumbling cathedral, a few pixels of that lumpen virtue now known as biodiversity.

So what is truly wild now? The child raised by wolves, the swelling oceans, weeds blowing through a derelict city, our genetics? Is not the global city now 'running wild' in its relentless pursuit of total environmental control? Paradoxically, the new wild is a matter of rationality as we start to appreciate the 'ecosystem services' that the old wild delivered for free. One thing is certain: wild is no longer simply a romantic counterpart to culture.

Certainly for our authors, incantations over the corpse of wild are vainglorious and premature. In this, the first issue of LA+ we find wild reimagined, resituated, and reconstituted. And for landscape architects this is important, because every line drawn and every word uttered is, in effect, an adjudication of just how wild things should be.

Tatum L. Hands
Editor in Chief

ADELA PARK

RE:

Adela Park is a graduate student at the University of Pennsylvania, pursuing a Masters of Landscape Architecture and a certificate in Historic Preservation. She holds a Bachelors of Metropolitan Studies from New York University.

+ CONSERVATION, GENETICS, ZOOLOGY, ECOLOGY

Two million years ago, the aurochs first appeared in India. One of the largest herbivores of its time (average bulls stood nearly six feet tall at the shoulders), *Bos primigenius* was a type of wild cattle that inhabited parts of Europe, Asia, and North Africa. During the Pleistocene epoch, the aurochs migrated, dispersed, and thrived. Popularly used in battle in Roman arenas, aurochs were later subject to excessive hunting by humans. In 1627, the last known aurochs died of natural causes in the Jaktorów Forest in Poland.[1] It was the world's first documented case of extinction.

The aurochs has, however, lived on in the imagination of biologists and ecologists. In the 1920s, prominent German biologists Lutz and Heinz Heck attempted to 'bring back' the aurochs. The result of their selective breeding experiments was the Heck cattle. While these animals do not genetically match the extinct aurochs, and only superficially resemble them, today nearly 600 of these creatures roam free at the Oostvaardersplassen, playing the role of aurochs in a large designated 'nature reserve' that attempts to recreate a Pleistocene ecosystem. This is just one of several projects to fall under the rubric of rewilding, a movement with origins in conservation biology but implications that range far wider. As more large-scale rewilding projects gain political and economic traction, ethical questions concerning our invention and reinvention of life forms come to the fore. Neither national parks nor parks for people, these rewilded landscapes also represent a new form of landscape architecture and as such call into question the agency of design in fabricating certain ideas of nature.

So what is 'rewilding', exactly? Its meaning and use have evolved from when it first emerged as a concept, referring quite literally to the release of captive animals back into the wild.[3] Its purview expanded to include the reintroduction of species, both plant and animal, into "habitats from which they had been excised."[4] More recently, the term has come to describe the restoration of entire ecosystems and the natural and ecological processes therein. As an approach to conservation, rewilding focuses on allowing ecological processes, rather than traditional management prescriptions, to shape or construct biological communities and ecosystems.[5] As Caroline Fraser explains:

> Rewilding was bold, urgent, new, radical. If existing links between parks and reserves could be exploited, fine. But if corridors were not available, they would have to be re-created. If that meant restoring damaged or destroyed forests or grasslands between them or reintroducing carnivores, then that is what had to be done.[6]

In the United States, the pioneering rewilding advocates included ecologists Michael Soulé and Reed Noss; David Johns, an attorney and environmentalist; Doug Tompkins, founder of North Face; and Dave Foreman, who later founded the Rewilding Institute.[7] Together, they launched the Wildlands Project and published "Plotting a North American Wilderness Recovery Strategy," a 1992 special issue of the magazine *Wild Earth*,[8] which contained plans for vast reserves and large networks of wildlands from the Adirondacks to the Rockies to the Great Smoky Mountains. These ideas filtered through the world of conservationists and biologists, eventually leading to ambitious plans such as the Yellowstone to Yukon Initiative (Y2Y), a vast continuous corridor now being implemented from the Greater Yellowstone ecoregion all the way to Canada's Yukon.[9] Y2Y became a catalyst for the rewilding movement in North America. Though it began with a single idea, it soon expanded to provide a network and organization for promoting various rewilding projects in both Canada and the United States. In addition to lobbying successfully for wildlife crossing structures in Banff, Y2Y cleared the path for a veritable "explosion of corridor planning across North America and around the world."[10] And once rewilding initiatives took hold internationally, they were characterized by an ever-widening vision, often continental in scale. Fraser identifies this as "perhaps the greatest effect of Y2Y...[it] inspired activists to be visionary, ambitious, even utopian."[11]

But while the American rewilding movement was gaining political momentum and making ambitious plans, Europe was already in the process of physically establishing major rewilding initiatives. Projects like the Oostvaardersplassen in the Netherlands and Pleistocene Park in northern Siberia have tested the ideas of rewilding with varying degrees of intentionality and control.

The Oostvaardersplassen, a 6,000-hectare nature reserve, sits just outside Amsterdam in the province of Flevoland. As a significant wetland ecosystem the Oostvaardersplassen emerged from the reclamation of the South Flevoland polder in 1968. Though originally intended for industrial use, a group of biologists persuaded the Dutch government to designate the area a nature reserve and Ramsar wetland, serving as the testing ground for the recreation of a Pleistocene landscape.[12] Thus, this reclaimed landscape came to be "a wilderness that was also constructed, Genesis-like, from the mud."[13]

Though not formally tied to the American political and environmental movement, the creation of the Oostvaardersplassen was influenced by rewilding's alternative conservation ethos. Elizabeth Kolbert has noted that "in the late seventies, the prevailing view in the Netherlands was—and, to a certain extent, still is—that nature was something to be managed, like a farm. According to this view, a preserve needed to be planted, pruned, and mowed, and the bigger the preserve, the more intervention was required."[14] Frans Vera, the Dutch ecologist leading the charge at the Oostvaardersplassen, particularly in respect to the introduction of Heck cattle, rejected this view of conservation management. "The problem, he decided, was that Europe's large grazers had been hunted to oblivion. If they could be restored, then nature could take care of itself."[15] Thus, the Oostvaardersplassen advocates a decidedly hands-off approach: "Unlike conventional conservation grazing systems in which herbivores are used as tools to achieve precise habitat targets, at the Oostvaardersplassen a policy of minimal intervention is practiced. The animals live on the reserve year-round and are free to breed and establish natural herd demography, social structures and behaviours."[16]

The animals that were given free range of habitat and behavior at the Oostvaardersplassen are meant to play the roles of species that would have inhabited the region in prehistoric times – had that area not in fact been engulfed by the North Sea. Heck cattle act as placeholders for the extinct aurochs, Konik ponies for the tarpan. In addition, red deer were brought in from Scotland and horses were imported from Poland. These species multiplied, and quickly. In the meantime, a variety of other animals began to populate the Oostvaardersplassen.[17] These animals included native and invasive species alike: foxes, muskrats, buzzards, goshawks, gray herons, kingfishers, kestrels, white-tailed eagles, and a rare black vulture. The numbers of these species fluctuated over the years, dependent on the available space and food supply. This rise and fall of the population cycle resulted in bursts of intense grazing, creating dynamic vegetation communities that occur with natural tree and shrub regeneration. In theory, human intervention is responsible only for the initial introduction of animals to the land; whatever subsequently occurs is the handiwork of nature itself. In this way, landscapes such as Oostvaardersplassen—created almost entirely by scientists—embody the very indeterminacy and self-organizational potential that has been so much a part of recent landscape architectural discourse. And yet, in the architecture of the Oostvaardersplassen landscape there is one species missing, namely the human.

Another rewilding project that aims to recreate a prehistoric ecosystem is "Pleistocene Park," created in 1989 by Russian ecologist and director of the Northeast Science Station Sergey A. Zimov. Zimov's project harkens back to an "epoch that supported vast populations of large animals including mammoths, horses, reindeer, bison, wolves, and other large predators."[18] Located in northern Siberia, Pleistocene Park is an ongoing project that tests the hypothesis that it was not a warming period that was responsible for the disappearance of large predators and mammoths, but "shifts in ecological dynamics wrought by people who relied on increasingly efficient hunting practices."[19] By recreating the mammoth steppe ecosystem and thus preserving and expanding areas of grassland, Zimov and his colleagues believe they can develop ways to mitigate the effects of global warming, and halt the release of carbon troves that are currently sequestered in the permafrost.

Zimov's stance on rewilding, however, goes further than merely reintroducing extant species, as is the case with the Oostvaardersplassen. Zimov is one of a group of scientists who believe that reviving extinct species plays an important role in increasing biological and genetic diversity, as well as the overall strength of ecosystems. De-extinction is a controversial process that has only been explored by the scientific community relatively recently. Nevertheless, there have been rapid advances in the technology of cloning and genomic engineering that make de-extinction a feasible reality.[20] Zimov's argument emphasizes the vital ecosystem services that were provided by large animals like the wooly mammoth: "The mammoths and numerous herbivores maintained the grassland by breaking up the soil and fertilizing it with their manure. Once they were gone, moss took over and transformed the grassland into less productive tundra."[21] Zimov is a strong supporter of work currently being undertaken to genetically engineer the revival of the wooly mammoth,[22] and would welcome the reintroduction of these long-gone mammals in Pleistocene Park.[23]

While Zimov's experiment might indeed enhance biodiversity and create an ecosystem in Siberia that sequesters more carbon, where does this logic stop? What is really interesting about rewilding is that it suggests that humans can now design landscapes genetically. As such, rewilding takes debates previously contained to 'designer babies' and literally sets them loose. Landscape design is no longer just the province of the landscape architect, the gardener or the farmer; it is rapidly becoming the province of the genetic engineer. As with the application of any technology, this is both frightening and beguiling.

1 Simon de Bruxelles, "A shaggy cow story: how a Nazi experiment brought extinct aurochs to Devon," *The Times* (2009).

2 George Monbiot, *Feral: Rewilding the Land, the Sea and Human Life* (Toronto: Penguin Group, 2013): 207.

3 Ibid, 8.

4 Ibid.

5 Birdlife International, "Rewilding may offer a sustainable alternative to traditional management" (2011) http://www.birdlife.org/datazone/sowb/casestudy/415.

6 Caroline Fraser, *Rewilding the World: Dispatches from the Conservation Revolution* (New York: Picador, 2009): 30.

7 Ibid., 32.

8 Ibid.

9 Ibid., 34.

10 Ibid., 37.

11 Ibid., 37-8.

12 Elizabeth Kolbert, "Recall of the Wild: The quest to engineer a world before humans," *The New Yorker* (2012): 50.

13 Ibid.

14 Ibid., 52.

15 Ibid.

16 Birdlife International, ibid.

17 Kolbert, "Recall of the Wild," 52.

18 Sergey A. Zimov, "Pleistocene Park: Return of the Mammoth's Ecosystem," *Science* 308 (2005): 796.

19 Ibid.

20 See, George Church & Ed Regis, *Regenesis: How Synthetic Biology Will Reinvent Nature and Ourselves* (New York: Basic Books, 2012).

21 Carl Zimmer, "Bringing Them Back to Life: The revival of an extinct species is no longer a fantasy. But is it a good idea?," *National Geographic* 223, no. 4 (2013).

22 Since 2012, South Korean and Russian researchers have been collaborating on a genomic engineering project to revive the wooly mammoth. For a discussion of the science behind this and other de-extinction projects, see Church & Regis, *Regenesis*.

23 Ibid.

RICHARD WELLER

WORLD P

Richard Weller is the Martin and Margy Meyerson Chair of Urbanism and Professor and Chair of Landscape Architecture at the University of Pennsylvania. He is also Adjunct Professor at the University of Western Australia and former Director of the Australian Urban Design Research Centre and the design firm Room 4.1.3.

➕ BIODIVERSITY, CONSERVATION, REGIONAL PLANNING, GOVERNANCE, ECOLOGY, MAPPING

IF GOD IS NOW 'GREEN'

and if Adam were to be evicted from paradise again, then his punishment would not be to convert wilderness into farms but farms back into wilderness. Eve, renowned for her scientific curiosity, would lead the way. And so it is—as E.O. Wilson wrote at the dawn of the 21st century—that the preservation and reconstruction of wilderness has become 'a universal moral imperative'.[1]

As semantically contradictory as the idea of cultivating wilderness is, that is exactly what governments, NGOs, scientists, and many well-intentioned citizens around the world are increasingly coming together to do. Greek groves, medieval forests, and modern national parks notwithstanding, for the first time in history humans are attempting, on a planetary scale, to reverse-engineer paradise. We now recognize that this is in our own best interests, but how we do it whilst simultaneously extracting more food and energy for an estimated global population of 10 billion is *the* big question.

The landscape we must begin with is an ecological hell: endless fields of chemically dependent monoculture, vermin, weeds, erosion, and the creeping desert forcing a diaspora toward coastal megacities. Interspersing these 'killing fields' of what is now routinely referred to as the Anthropocene era or the Sixth Extinction, are the fragmentary remnants of global habitat – embattled arks into which what is left of the world's once-munificent biodiversity is now huddled.

Opposite: "The Creation of the World and the Expulsion from Paradise," by Giovanni di Paolo.

Otherwise known as protected areas, these refuges are categorized by the International Union for the Conservation of Nature (IUCN) along a sliding scale from the pristine "strictly protected and unmodified" at one end, to places where humans actively engage in the optimistic and somewhat malleable ideal of "sustainable resource management" at the other.[2] Imagining the IUCN's organization of ecological space as a horizontal version of Dante's organization of spiritual space, then we can safely assume that category one is Eden while category six is purgatory. The unclassified rest–the wastelands of urbanism's planetary infrastructure–are lands the ecological community now politely refers to as novel ecology.[3]

For the novel ecosystem–defined as nature irrevocably changed by humans–there is, quite literally, no way back. The novel ecosystem is unknown territory: a place where the old epistemological bedrock of Nature is no more, and as such one can only *fall* into the future.[4] Of course, we could argue that since human activity is by now ubiquitous, all the IUCN's lands are novel, but there is no need to rehearse pristine nature's well-known fall from grace here: what I want to do is explore the mongrel lands in between and ask how landscape architecture might find redemption; how we might now go to work on a scale commensurate with that of biodiversity's otherwise inexorable decline? As Erle Ellis writes, "[t]he critical challenge is in maintaining, enhancing and restoring the ecological functions of the remnant, recovering, and managed novel ecosystems formed by land use and its legacies within the complex multifunctional anthropogenic landscape mosaics that are the predominant form of terrestrial ecosystems today and into the future."[4]

The key to this lies in the law of the land, specifically the interpretation and application of three key terms in the United Nations' Convention on Biological Diversity (CBD). The first is that for the 194 nations that are party to the CBD,[5] the Convention sets a target of securing 17% of the earth's terrestrial areas as protected habitat by 2020. The second is that this land cannot just be anywhere: it must be "ecologically representative." And the third is that these lands should be "well connected."[6] To be truly representative, future protected areas must by definition be distributed across the world's 867 recognized ecoregions. Furthermore, to be truly well connected, they would need to be linked together across myriad jurisdictional boundaries and infrastructural lines so as to form a continuous global matrix.

Presently, protected lands for all types of habitat are unevenly distributed across 235 countries in 160,000 fragmented sites. As biologist Dan Janzen often points out, unless they are very big fragments, these refugia are ultimately useless in terms of long-term biological productivity.[7] Taken as a whole, these sites constitute 13% of the world's remaining unadulterated habitat and represent little more than half of earth's ecoregions. The CBD requirement that another 4% be secured by 2020 might, on first impression, seem paltry but 4% of the earth's terrestrial surface is 5,932,000 km2, the equivalent of over 1.73 million

Central Parks. That's a linear park 6.92 million kilometers long (0.8 km wide) stretching 1,726 times around the world!

Literally growing out of the conservation achievements of previous centuries the best-known large-scale contemporary conservation effort today is probably that of the Yellowstone to Yukon (Y2Y) project.[8] Founded in 1993, Y2Y is a complex cultural and political phenomenon, one that aims to amalgamate and secure some 3,200 km of land (much of which is IUCN categories 1 and 2) along America's northwestern and Canada's southwestern mountainous spine. Y2Y is a model project because of its scale, complexity and sustained effort to create connectivity on a continental scale. As a predominantly mountainous landscape it is also looked to as inspiration for other high-altitude landscapes around the world into which species will inevitably migrate as global warming continues.[9]

Similar initiatives for the creation of large-scale connectivity to ensure the flow of species' gene pools over time are underway elsewhere in the United States and beyond. For example, the Algonquin to Adirondacks project is trying to achieve 400 km of connected habitat on the United States east coast and, in Australia, the Great Eastern Ranges Initiative involves some 2,800 km of connected mountainous habitat along that continent's east coast. Other projects of equal ambition are being planned in Bhutan, the Himalayas, Africa, Central and South America, and from Lisbon to Kiev; indeed, the Pan-European Ecological Network (PEEN) aims to interconnect all of Europe.[10]

Pre-eminent in this regard are the Dutch who have been actively planning and constructing a national ecological network of protected areas and "robust corridors" since 1990.[11] This national planning is supported by a 'defragmentation plan', which addresses the specifics of how ecological corridors transcend jurisdictional boundaries and physical impediments to linking existing fragments of habitat. Although small, rich and culturally inclined towards such rational planning, the Dutch example is exemplary because it is not just about linking remote areas of mountainous wilderness, but rather about reorganizing an entirely novel, national ecosystem so that urbanism, agriculture, and biodiversity can coexist in a mutually beneficial manner.

In 2001 Graham Bennett and Piet Witt reported to the IUCN that there were at least 150 active ecological network projects of a landscape or regional scale active around the world and no doubt there are now many more.[12] However, unlike the Dutch (who not only have a national, well-financed plan, but also a plan that is nested within the superstructure of the PEEN), an overwhelming majority of the 194 nations who are party to the CBD 2020 targets have no semblance of spatial planning. And where they do, they tend to simply consist of thick green lines or fuzzy airbrushed zones superimposed over maps at a scale so big as to be meaningless.

Although generally for aesthetic, rather than ecological purposes, in the early to mid-20th century the first landscapes to form linear connections in cities such as London and Stockholm were known as 'greenbelts'. Due to urban pressures, greenbelts morphed into thinner recreational and storm-water retention strips threaded through burgeoning suburbia. Tracing unbuildable drainage lines and ridgelines or buffering incompatible land uses, these often excessively large public spaces typically lack biological complexity and social investment and as such are susceptible to invasive species and degrade into ecological oblivion.

Precedents more relevant to the scale of today's global aim to connect fragmentary habitats include easements along railways, canals, and later freeways: all of which go some way, albeit unintentionally, to supporting slithers of biodiversity. More deliberate and indeed visionary was Benton Mackaye's Appalachian trail of 1921 – a scenic route stretching 3,379 km from Georgia to Maine and a conduit along which massive conservation efforts in both the Southern and North Appalachians continue to this day. The East Coast Greenway, conceived to run 4,800 km along the entire eastern seaboard of the United States, now parallels the Appalachian Trail. Pilgrimage routes and hiking trails of this dimension are increasingly popular the world over and when coupled with planning for habitat protection and connectivity to support species migration they can form important cultural and ecological linkages.

In landscape architectural theory and practice today, large-scale linear landscapes are generically referred to as 'greenways'. According to long-time researcher and advocate of greenways Jack Ahern, the prototypical modern greenway system was the United States' Wisconsin Heritage trail, some 300 km of connected landscape corridors designed by Phil Lewis in 1964.[13] Greenways were given the imprimatur of the White House in 1987, when The President's Commission on Americans Outdoors declared that they should thread "through cities and countrysides like a giant circulation system" and "give every American easy access to the natural world."[14] As a consequence, writing in 2006 Paul Hellmund and Daniel Smith estimated that in the United States alone there were over 3,000 greenways.[15] Contemporary greenways projects typically occur at the metropolitan scale, though sometimes, as in Florida and Maryland, they can reach statewide or, as is the case with New England's Greenway Vision Plan, across several states. As the Fabos Conference on Landscape and Greenway Planning attests, the theory and practice of designing these systems is now a mature and vibrant international movement.[16]

In their survey of what is now meant by the use of the term greenways, Hellmund and Smith list 30 different typologies ranging from continental-scale wildlife corridors to mere bio-swales in suburban developments.[17] In an effort to be more definitive, Ahern writes that greenways are "networks of land that are planned, designed and managed for multiple purposes

1 Edward O. Wilson, *The Creation: An Appeal to Save Life on Earth* (New York: WW. Norton and Co., 2006), 99.

2 IUCN, "Protected Area Categories," http://www.iucn.org/about/work/programmes/gpap_home/gpap_quality/gpap_pacategories/ (accessed 26 June 2014).

3 Novel ecosystems are defined as "a system of abiotic, biotic and social components (and their interactions) that, by virtue of human influence, differ from those that prevailed historically, having a tendency to self-organize and manifest novel qualities without intensive human management. Novel ecosystems are distinguished from hybrid ecosystems by practical limitations (a combination of ecological, environmental and social thresholds) on the recovery of historical qualities." Richard J. Hobbs, E. Higgs & C. Hall, *Novel Ecosystems: Intervening in the New Ecological World Order* (Hoboken, NJ: Wiley-Blackwell, 2013), 58.

4 Erle C. Ellis, "Anthropogenic Taxonomies: A Taxonomy of the Human Biosphere," in Chris Reed & Nina-Marie Lister (eds), *Projective Ecologies* (New York: Actar Publishers, 2014), 179.

5 Convention on Biological Diversity (CBD), "List of Parties," http://www.cbd.int/information/parties.shtml (accessed 26 June 2014).

6 CBD, "Aichi Target 11 Technical Rationale," http://www.cbd.int/sp/targets/rationale/target-11/ (accessed 20 July 2013).

7 Daniel Janzen, "Gardenification of Wildland Nature and the Human Footprint," *Science* 279, no. 5355 (1998): 1312–1313.

8 Yellowstone to Yukon Conservation Initiative, http://y2y.net/ (accessed 20 July 2014).

9 For a description of the Y2Y project see Harvey Locke, "Yellowstone to Yukon Connectivity Conservation Initiative" in Graeme Worboys et al. (eds), *Connectivity Conservation Management: Global Guide* (London: Earthscan, 2010), 161–181.

10 Kalle Remm et al., Design of the "Pan-European Ecological Network: A National Level Attempt," in Rob Jongman & Gloria Pugnetti (eds), *Ecological Networks and Greenways: Concept, Design, Implementation* (New York: Cambridge Studies in Landscape Ecology, 2004), 151–170.

11 Rob Jongman Rob & Marion Bogers, "Current Status of the Practical Implementation of Ecological Networks in the Netherlands," European Centre for Nature Conservation, 2008.

12 G. Bennett and P. Witt, "The Development and Application of Ecological Networks: A Review of Proposals, Plans and Programs," IUCN Report B1142 (Gland Switzerland: World Conservation Union and AID Environment, 2001).

13 Jack Ahern, "Greenways in the USA: Theory, Trends and Prospects," in Jongman & Pugnetti (eds), *Ecological Networks and Greenways*, 39.

14 *The President's Commission on Americans Outdoors*, Report (1987), 102.

15 Paul Hellmund & Daniel Smith, *Designing Greenways: Sustainable Landscapes for Nature and People* (Washington: Island Press, 2006), 32.

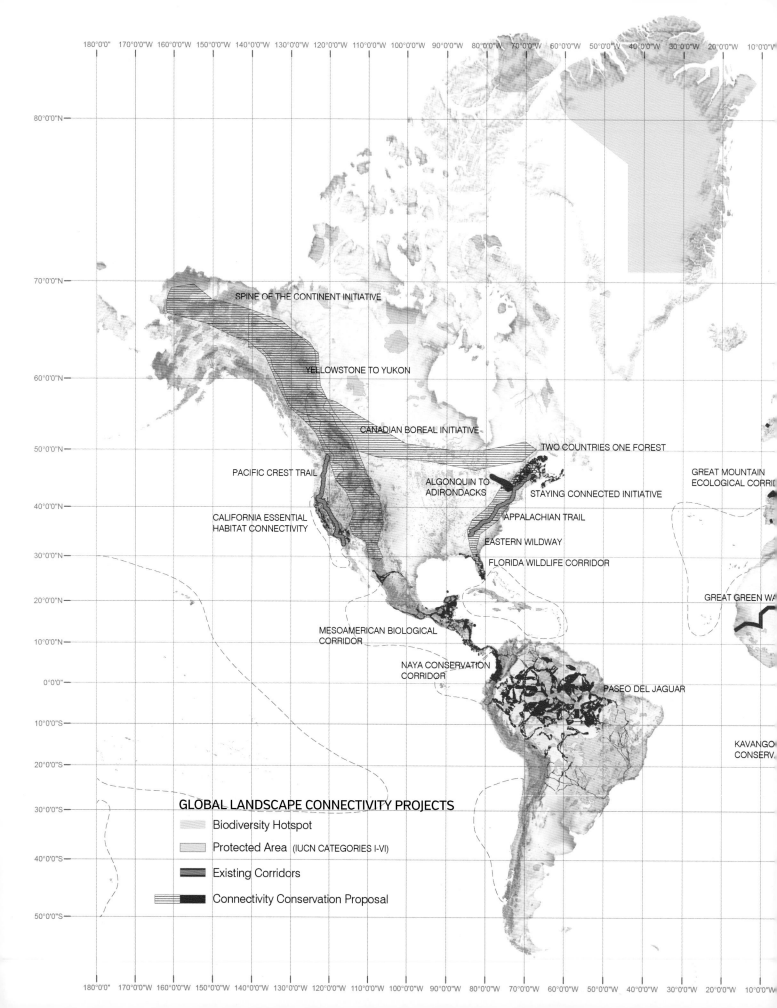

GLOBAL LANDSCAPE CONNECTIVITY PROJECTS

Biodiversity Hotspot

Protected Area (IUCN CATEGORIES I-VI)

Existing Corridors

Connectivity Conservation Proposal

SPINE OF THE CONTINENT INITIATIVE

YELLOWSTONE TO YUKON

CANADIAN BOREAL INITIATIVE

TWO COUNTRIES ONE FOREST

PACIFIC CREST TRAIL

ALGONQUIN TO ADIRONDACKS

STAYING CONNECTED INITIATIVE

GREAT MOUNTAIN ECOLOGICAL CORRI

CALIFORNIA ESSENTIAL HABITAT CONNECTIVITY

APPALACHIAN TRAIL

EASTERN WILDWAY

FLORIDA WILDLIFE CORRIDOR

GREAT GREEN WA

MESOAMERICAN BIOLOGICAL CORRIDOR

NAYA CONSERVATION CORRIDOR

PASEO DEL JAGUAR

KAVANGO CONSERV.

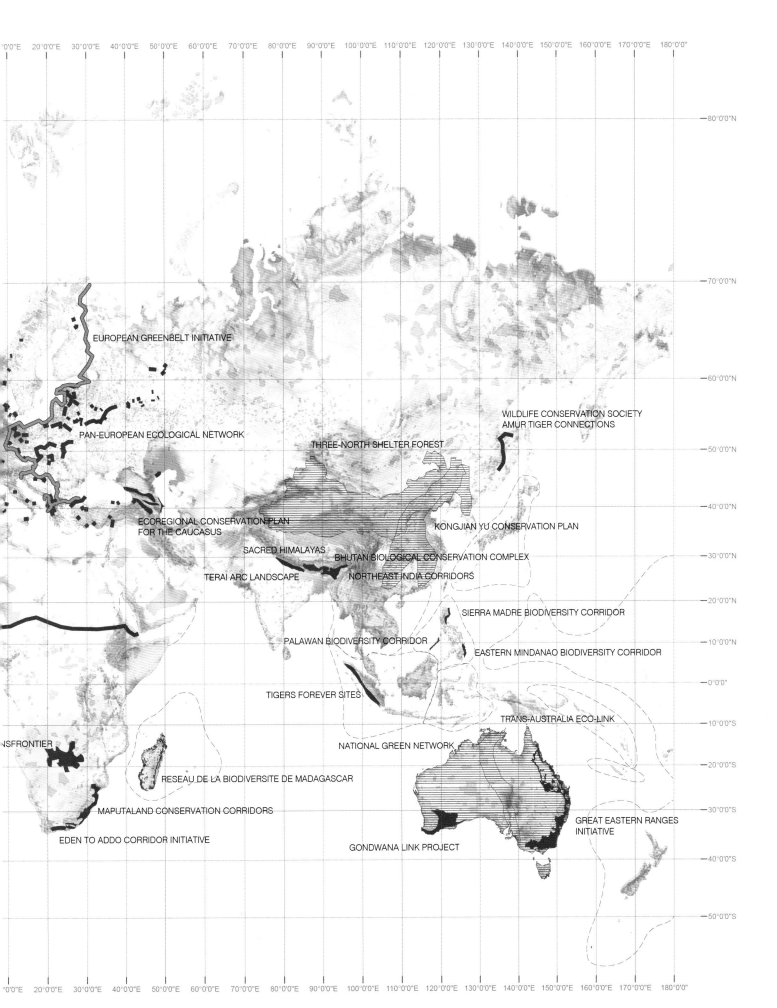

EUROPEAN GREENBELT INITIATIVE

WILDLIFE CONSERVATION SOCIETY
AMUR TIGER CONNECTIONS

PAN-EUROPEAN ECOLOGICAL NETWORK

THREE-NORTH SHELTER FOREST

ECOREGIONAL CONSERVATION PLAN
FOR THE CAUCASUS

KONGJIAN YU CONSERVATION PLAN

SACRED HIMALAYAS

BHUTAN BIOLOGICAL CONSERVATION COMPLEX

TERAI ARC LANDSCAPE

NORTHEAST INDIA CORRIDORS

SIERRA MADRE BIODIVERSITY CORRIDOR

PALAWAN BIODIVERSITY CORRIDOR

EASTERN MINDANAO BIODIVERSITY CORRIDOR

TIGERS FOREVER SITES

TRANS-AUSTRALIA ECO-LINK

NATIONAL GREEN NETWORK

NSFRONTIER

RESEAU DE LA BIODIVERSITE DE MADAGASCAR

MAPUTALAND CONSERVATION CORRIDORS

GREAT EASTERN RANGES
INITIATIVE

EDEN TO ADDO CORRIDOR INITIATIVE

GONDWANA LINK PROJECT

including ecological, recreational, cultural aesthetic, or other purposes compatible with the concept of sustainable land-use."[18] In short, greenways have become all things to all people and confusion arises because where American landscape architects use the term 'greenways', European planners tend to refer to 'ecological networks' and conservationists to 'wildlife corridors'.

I argue greenways, ecological networks, and wildlife corridors are best understood as gradations of a contiguous system ranging in scale from the former to the latter respectively. In this schema, greenways are generally the smallest in scale yet have the highest human presence and involve the highest level of design so as to serve multiple functions. Ecological networks such as that in Holland (or the PEEN) is a term I think best applied to the bioregional, state, or national scale, and invariably requires exceptional political will and design/planning negotiations so as to traverse jurisdictional boundaries and cross established agricultural landscapes. The third term, wildlife corridors, refers primarily to connecting protected areas for species dispersal and migration and their scale and level of design is a function of the distance and level of hindrance between the protected areas and the specific needs of the species in question.

In the landscape architecture program at the University of Pennsylvania we are conducting a mapping exercise which scopes the scale of ecological networks for the 425 ecoregions which make up the world's 35 biodiversity hotspots[19] if these regions were to meet the CBD target of 17% protected and connected habitat. This project aims to establish accurate base maps of each ecoregion and determine the shortfall between its current protected areas and the CBD (Aichi) target. These are base maps from which nations, regions, and communities can begin to spatially understand what is involved in meeting the targets. As such, they are open to interpretation: on the one hand showing the crudeness of global policy settings or, on the other, encouraging nations to 'look for land' that can be wrested from development and 'given' to biodiversity.

So where can nations find this land? With the aid of GIS modeling systems and population biology analysis, least-cost maximum-biodiversity options for connecting fragmented habitat can be projected.[20] In the first instance it is landscape ecologists in consultation with local communities who should advise where the main lines of connectivity should run, but it is landscape architects who are best positioned to help negotiate how these lines interact with the complexity of the whole landscape.

The creation of greenways on continental scales is then a project of immense cultural, political, and entrepreneurial imagination. As Dan Janzen explains, to do this we need to move beyond the image of pure wilderness and cultivate large areas of new wildlands as if they were gardens – places which have "all the traits that we have long bestowed on a garden including care, planning, investment, zoning, insurance, fine tuning, research and premeditated harvest."[21]

World Park

If National Parks were the crowning conservation achievement of the 19th and 20th centuries, reflecting a time when nation-states were the predominant political unit, then surely the IUCN's ever-increasing list of protected areas amounts to a new form of 'World Park' borne of 21st-century global culture. Be that as it may, the 'hotspots' in which the world's most valuable and most threatened biodiversity is corralled remain fragmented both within and across national borders and are highly vulnerable to the geo-political contingencies of sovereign rule.

What then, if in accordance with the CBD's 2020 (Aichi) targets we were to consider linking the world's most biodiverse and threatened landscapes into one contiguous World Park – replete with appropriate governance and funding to not only protect but now reconnect what remains? Two continuous routes stand out: one running north–south from Alaska to Patagonia and the other east–west from Indonesia to Morocco. Continuous trails in these locations could practically and symbolically interlink a large proportion of the world's most biodiverse and most threatened landscapes. These trails could catalyze global cooperation and environmental investment attracting people not only wanting to visit remaining fragments of wilderness, but also (and more importantly) to help augment connections between fragments along the way. The relatively simple idea of these two trails could help in galvanizing and focusing a landscape reclamation project on a scale commensurate with the crisis. Of course, these two paradisiacal axes are wildly improbable, but then so too is every other form of global connectivity humans have constructed since they left The Garden.

16 J. Fábos et al. (eds), "Proceedings of Fábos Conference on Landscape and Greenway Planning 2013: Pathways to Sustainability," University of Massachusetts, Amherst, April 12–13, 2013.

17 Hellmund & Smith, *Designing Greenways*.

18 Jack Ahern, "Greenways as a Planning Strategy," in J. Fábos and J. Ahern (eds), *Greenways: The Beginning of a Movement* (Amsterdam: Elsevier, 1996), 131–55.

19 See, Russell Mittermeier et al., *Hotspots Revisited: Earth's Biologically Richest and Most Endangered Terrestrial Ecoregions* (Washington: Conservation International and Cemex, 2004) furthering research fist published by Norman Meyers in 1988. In 2010 a 35th Hotspot (The Forests of East Australia) was identified: Kristen Williams et al, "Ecological Society of Australia 2010 Annual Conference: Sustaining Biodiversity – the next 50 years," *Conference Handbook* (Canberra: Ecological Society of Australia, 2010).

20 Deborah A. Rudnick et al., "The Role of Landscape Connectivity in Planning and Implementing Conservation and Restoration Priorities," *Issues in Ecology* 16 (2012).

21 Janzen, "Gardenification of Wildland Nature and the Human Footprint," 1313.

World Park

NORTH-SOUTH CORRIDOR

2 continents

13 countries

~25,000 kilometers

>2 years to walk

Pacific Crest Trail

California Coastal Trail

Yosemite National Park

Juan Bautista de Anza Trail

El Camino Real de
Tierra Adentro Trail

Monarch Butterfly Reserve

Tikal National Park

TransPanama Trail

Area de Conservacion Guanacaste

Darien National Park

Machu Picchu

Qhapaq Nan
Main Andean Road

Los Glacieres National Park

Donana National Park

M

—— Existing Trail

---- Proposed Connection

Biodiversity Hotspot

Protected Area (IUCN categories 1-4)

Protected Area (IUCN categories 5-6)

● World Heritage Site

○ Border Crossing

kilometers

0   500 1,000   2,000   3,000   4,000

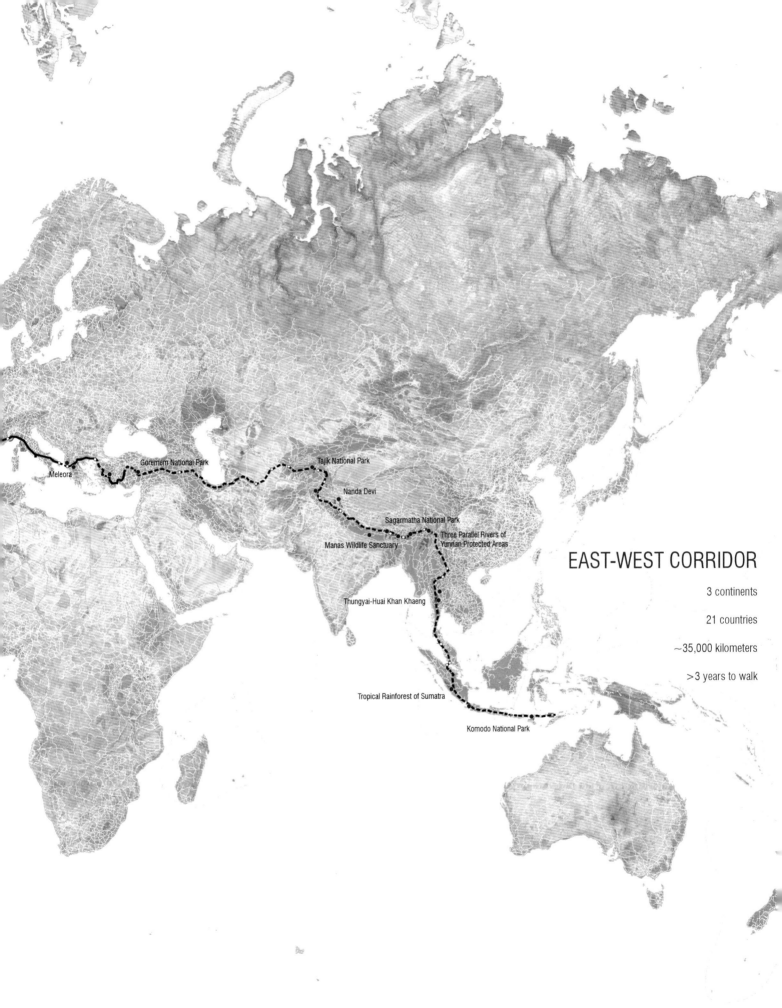

Meleora

Goremem National Park

Tajik National Park

Nanda Devi

Sagarmatha National Park

Three Parallel Rivers of
Yunnan Protected Areas

Manas Wildlife Sanctuary

Thungyai-Huai Khan Khaeng

Tropical Rainforest of Sumatra

Komodo National Park

EAST-WEST CORRIDOR

3 continents

21 countries

~35,000 kilometers

>3 years to walk

IN CONVERSATION WITH
DAN JANZEN & WINNIE HALLWACHS

✛ BIOLOGY, ECOLOGY, CONSERVATION, LANDSCAPE ECONOMICS

Biologists Dan Janzen and Winnie Hallwachs have devoted their last 29 years to researching and protecting biological diversity in Costa Rica. Their long-term vision and engagement with local politics and real estate have helped to transform the 20,000-hectare Parque Nacional Santa Rosa, established in 1971, into the Área de Conservación Guanacaste (ACG) of today: 165,000 hectares of protected and uninterrupted tropical ecosystems, home to approximately 375,000 species of plants and animals.

An environmental impact study of gold miners squatting on protected parklands in the Parque Nacional Corcovado in 1985 helped shape their philosophy of the importance of deeply involving Costa Rican residents and economies in the survival of their wild biodiversity. Over the following decades, the husband-and-wife team facilitated growth and management strategies for ACG that include bioliteracy programs for local elementary schools, employment opportunities for local residents, a resident staff, and partnerships with agricultural and resource extraction interests. In 2014, Dan and the Instituto Nacional de Biodiversidad (which he and Winnie helped found) were jointly awarded the prestigious Blue Planet Prize by the Asahi Glass Foundation for "outstanding achievements in scientific research and its application that have helped to provide solutions to global environmental problems."

+ You argue for large patches of land, 50,0000-150,000 hectares. What is your view on landscape connectivity, the idea of corridors?

D Corridors are absolute bullshit.

W Ohhh! Maybe we could...maybe we could soften that.

D Corridors are a myth generated by the conservation community on a blackboard because they look nice. They have this piece here and this piece there. "Oh! We'll have a strip of land..." But, organisms don't flow like water. If you want to save this piece and you want to save this piece, you buy all the junk in between and make it one big piece and let it regenerate. But, you see, that didn't sit well with the conservation community for several reasons. One is because you're going to have take care of all that land, and the other is that the land in between often doesn't look like much to start with. It's often little fields, pastures, and such. But we come from the position that over time it regenerates, and we don't care if it takes 100–300 years. We're not in it for what kind of glory we can get today to impress some donor who will then give us more money so we can have a bigger overhead and a three-storey building in Washington, DC...our goal is to save the biodiversity. That's our goal. It's not to have a big NGO. It's not to employ a thousand people in offices who have salaries. Those aren't our goals.

W I think there are some genuine people who want to save biodiversity–but who have a small list of species in mind–who are legitimately interested in corridors. I don't think it has to be painted with such a scathing brush.

D Well, that's true. The conservation people got suckered with this word 'corridor.' So then they plan like crazy and they draw all these maps with all the little lines and say, 'See, we solved the problem: we've got 164 pieces of Costa Rican land conserved and they're connected by corridors.' And they draw a little thin strip like this and then you end up with the question, what's actually happening in the corridor? We don't actually know, but there it is on the map. Nothing there, and nothing ever will be there except agroscape. Ask someone how to improve the chances that the biodiversity of some large area will survive the next millennium, and he won't say to use the money to promote corridors. He or she will say, expand the area to include more diversity and area of ecosystems and habitats.

+ Do you think the designation of the world's biodiversity hotspots has been a good thing for raising global awareness and focusing funding streams to places that need it the most?

W If you needed to make a decision about where would you put the money, the key question of whether it would be socially possible in such and such a place would be a major factor.

D Exactly. Whether it's socially possible and whether you still have something there to worry over. The exercise of planning conservation for Honduras is ridiculous. You have money to spend on conservation in Honduras? Fine, tell me how much it is. You get three people that know the biology of Honduras and they can tell you in one week with one helicopter where that money should be spent.

+ The movement of rewilding large parts of the US seems to be gaining some currency. Do you hold out any hope for large-scale landscape projects as a way for restoring the world's ecosystems?

D I don't think it's gaining any currency at all. I think it's fashionable to talk about it. I don't view that as currency. For God's sake, we don't have to rewild anything! You've got elephants and rhinos in Africa; they're all endangered like crazy. Are we going to bring them over here and turn them wild in Wyoming and Kansas and Oklahoma and just see how long this society tolerates their presence? And how are these things going to exist? Well, we're rewilding the western United States from Yukon to Wyoming, or Yukon to Kansas or wherever the hell it is. This is all just hyperbole produced by people who are raising attention for themselves. Now there are big projects; there's a thing called the American Prairie Foundation who are buying up big chunks of terrain to turn them back into what the national parks should have been in the first place. That's fine, but that's not rewilding. US society has no interest in turning seriously large areas back to the animals and plants that once occupied them. How compatible is Iowa and Kansas with free-ranging elephants and rhinos?

+ How do you see frozen zoos and frozen seed banks in relation to your own work?

D Well, I long had in my mind a dichotomy between what I call a green freezer and a brown freezer. A green freezer is a big chunk of wild area that you know well enough so you can find stuff when you want, but it's there reproducing, doing its own thing (and even evolving). The brown freezer is a seed bank and that requires of course that you know what's in the gene(s) and how to get it out and grow it. It has its maintenance cost: you have to regrow the seeds and harvest them again and put them in every 10 years or whatever, depending on what you're doing. But so does the wild area have a maintenance cost. Each one has maintenance costs; each one does different things. I don't see them as necessarily as either/or...I can see why the crop people who want to keep genes for better sorghum or better corn keep a seed bank for that purpose. I don't think in any way that represents a wild area. I see the seed bank and frozen tissue and that kind of stuff as pragmatic human beings storing for their own direct use, whereas I see the wild area as having that function, and also intrinsic value as a wild area.

W One dollar for corridors, two dollars for big areas – fine. But when it's all out of the same pot. And the same is true for the people who want to bring back the mammoth. Fine. When the other things are being taken care of, but not over and over again, with people who love to be on front covers of magazines...for being people with brand new ideas on the cutting edge. They all say, 'We do this, people will get excited, money will flow into conservation."

D It doesn't.

W Very small chance. Very, very small chance. Now it is a lovely idea, but not one that should be our goal. It should be very peripheral.

D The world in which those animals existed, the ones that they want to bring back, that world is no longer here. People say, well we can reproduce the passenger pigeon. No, I'm sorry, you can't. That requires hundreds of thousands of square miles of oak trees and we don't have hundreds of thousands of square miles of oak trees anymore, and no one is going to give them back to you or the passenger pigeon. That was Michigan and Wisconsin and Indiana and Pennsylvania and Illinois. And that's it. If it's going to be anything, it will be a crop pest. And it will descend on your corn crop and your wheat crop and some day we'll be out there shooting them like other crop pests. Again, you cannot even keep the elephant and rhino populations alive in their own ecosystems, and they want to put a mammoth population back into California?

+ Biodiversity has been more or less wiped out before in history by natural events and over time it re-emerges. How is human destruction of biodiversity different?

D Basically because we don't give the world back after we destroy it. You see, what happens is the volcano or the hurricane or the tsunami that goes around the world three times after the meteorite hit off the top of Yucatan – after that it gave something, gave the world back to biodiversity. That's why you're here. That thing 65 million years ago took the dinosaurs off the planet, but it left an open playing field for all these things to re-evolve and re-emerge. What we're doing is turning it all into alfalfa and parking lots. So our goal isn't to give it back. That's the real difference. That's not what people emphasize. They emphasize the loss of this or that species. I think that's a very poor strategy. I don't think most people give a damn whether biodiversity goes, and certainly do not care about some rat living in a South American rainforest. The problem lies in people having no bioliteracy. They have no idea what's going down the drain, so they don't care. Why should they care? So you tell them 100,000 species are going to go extinct in the next 10 years and...so what? How will that impact them, personally? The other piece of it is, we are in an engineered artificial emergency here. We've been doing this for better than 10,000 years. We've been soiling our nest and wiping the stuff off for a very long time. That is what humans do. They eliminate the 'wild' to make room for humans and their domesticates, and nature pushes back. And finally nature has lost the pushing contest.

Opposite: Costa Rican moths and butterflies, reared from wild-caught caterpillars in Area de Conservación Guanacaste by native parataxonomists. The insects are now part of the Smithsonian Institution permanent archives.

+ Some scientists support assisted migration of species in relation to climate change and some do not. What side of this debate do you come down on?

D Depends. You have a particular species that you want to save and there are different ways to save it. And bear in mind, every time you move a species somewhere you're interfering with the guys who are already there. So what you're doing is creating an invasive species. So, where's your value judgement? You have to decide. Do you want elephants or do you not want elephants? Turn 'em loose in Kansas, that's my solution. What I think is particularly fun is everyone wants to think about migrating species to avoid climate change. All right, why don't we talk about migrating species to save them, period? Let's put elephants into Yellowstone. Elephants would do gorgeous in Yellowstone. And a whole lot of other things, along with the wolves and the grizzly bears. No problem whatsoever. Rhinos probably would do well too. There's all kinds of stuff we could save by moving it to some other place on the planet.

W Well...I think, Dan's actually not at all [laughs] advising this!

D Why not? Elephants? They went all the way to the top of Mt Kilimanjaro. No problem; no problem at all.

+ Are you worried about climate change?

W Yes.

D Am I worried about climate change? No, because, of course, it's happening. There's nothing to worry about, it's just there. It's happening. It's been happening, it's not a new thing for us. It's the last 20 years plus; probably more than that if we were paying attention, but certainly the last 20 years it has been very obvious. But what would worry do? I like to think of ourselves as doing something about a problem, not worrying about it. We have worked to purchase land to expand national parks, partly as an amelioration for climate change, because we can see our stuff moving from one ecosystem to another. One of the various rationales for purchasing more land was to give more space and ecosystems to move into. And to make that a better lifeboat in the face of life – of climate change. But I don't think we worry about it. We simply see it happening and where we have the economic ability to buy a piece of land to try to ameliorate it, we do it.

+ Have you ever worked with landscape architects in planning the development and management of Guanacaste?

For more information on Área de Conservación Guanacaste visit www.acguanacaste.ac.cr

D We are landscape architects. I think anybody that designs, or works toward the design of a significant conservation area is, by definition, a landscape architect. What is architecture? It's design. Well we are designing a wild area, if only by the fact of which pieces of land we buy up to the fact of where they put the roads and where they put the buildings. It is whether they decide to buy this piece versus that piece. And that's no different than designing the landscape of a city or a city park or anything like that. We had an interesting specific case that happened on a particular little national park we started in: Parque Nacional Santa Rosa. There was a big piece of property at the north boundary, which early conservation in the 70s fingered immediately to include [in the national park]. There was no boundary between these two properties, so we ended up having to define the boundary. It's on the map, but you have to actually figure out where it is. So I go out there and I start exploring this boundary as it is on a map and as I'm going along and I suddenly realize this boundary was not put in by a landowner. Because every time we got to a place where there was an interesting piece of habitat, the boundary went around it and captured it. And then it went on again; and then did the same thing. So you get this wiggly boundary. The only sense I can make out of this is whoever made this boundary was a biologist. So I started poking backwards and it turned out it was a bird-watcher friend [Bob Jenkins] of a bunch of Peace Corps volunteers who visited from Turrialba on the other side of Costa Rica. And it made total sense then, because you could see what he had done to get the biologically good habitat included in the new park. So the business of conservation is, to me, a de facto act of landscape architecture.

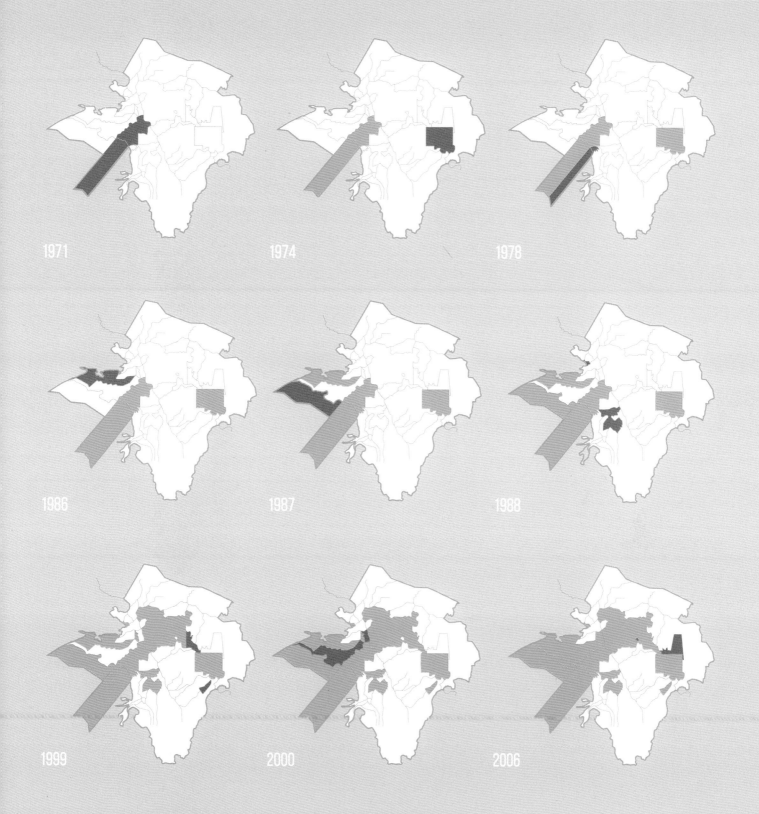

1971   1974   1978

1986   1987   1988

1999   2000   2006

GROWTH OF THE GUANACASTE CONSERVATION AREA
NEW ACQUISITION ●
EXISTING PARKLANDS ●

PAUL CARTER
TRACKING WILDERNESS: THE ARCHITECTURE OF INSCAPES

Paul Carter is Professor of Design (Urbanism) in the Design Research Institute at RMIT University, Australia. He is the author of 15 books on history, art, and design including *The Road to Botany Bay: An essay in spatial history* (1987), *Material Thinking* (2004) and *Dark Writing: Geography, Performance, Design* (2008). As an artist he has been involved in the design of a number of public spaces in Australia, including Federation Square (Melbourne). He visited the Lupunaluz site in December 2012.

╬ ANTHROPOLOGY, CULTURAL STUDIES

The paradox of connection informs every aspect of wildness. Wilderness, at least as Richard Weller documents elsewhere in this issue, is redefined in terms of connected linear regions. Connectivity is understood ecologically as a management technique for the maintenance of biodiversity across habitats and climes. In terms of frontier-mentality land settlement practices, the development of new wild corridors implies a limit to connectivity. A network of biodiversity greenways represents a clear obstacle to the plan to reduce the world to a uniform grid of agricultural, industrial, and residential functions. But how can such global reconnections—with their politically perilous attempt to redefine connecting as relating—be absorbed into local initiatives? How, in the other direction, does a project, inevitably defined by the colonial survey, reach out to this larger scale of reintegration? The following notes reflect on this challenge in the context of Lupunaluz, a nature retreat, healing center, and educational program in development in the Peruvian rainforest southeast of Iquitos, at the headwaters of the Amazon basin.

Like many cultural and biodiversity initiatives, Lupunaluz understands the importance of developing a network of rainforest corridors. Its Australian-US founders are highly conscious of the complexities of developing sustainable and equable business arrangements with local communities. They readily embrace holistic understandings of the relationship between body, spirit, and place—and accept the regional Shipibo view that human–nonhuman communication is both possible and desirable—but are acutely alive to the challenge of terminological fatigue. Besides, it is naïve to envisage a post-wildness community of interests emerging (through creative residencies, through shamanic healing rituals, through various forms of knowledge transfer and cross-cultural education) when the Shipibo themselves cannot be stereotyped; as displaced, postcolonial people whose worldview is markedly Manichean[1] and who, until recently, performed initiation rituals that outsiders found difficult to rationalize, they are bearers of privileged insight into the interconnectedness of sentient life forms profoundly embedded in the twinned traumas of economic and cultural despoliation.

However, cultural relativism apart, the Shipibo peoples do in one profoundly challenging way dissolve the nature–culture divide. In contrast with western cultures, they derive human consciousness from plant consciousness. This radical inversion of what we in the west might call a landscape sensibility goes in some ways beyond traditional animistic understandings of human–nonhuman linkages. Through the conduit of the *ayahuasca* ceremony, and the mediation of the shaman, the trees speak, or at least make manifest their will. The rainforest trees communicate directly with the brain; indeed activate the tree within human consciousness. The visions that mediate this information are of designs, mandala-like diagrams that can be construed as energy materializations flowing throughout the body-spirit-environment and binding all parts together. The implication the Lupunaluz project draws from this is that the design of the proposed center (the building morphologies, locations, and arrangements, together with the associated gardens, tracks, meeting places, and public–private zones) is critical to the affective qualities of care and balance that it wants to communicate.

But how is this to be done? An intensive examination of the site is occurring as this article is written. It is iterative as different sensory, customary, and technical knowledges of the environment and its human uses are amalgamated into spatial patterns suggestive of energy distributions scientifically measurable on the ground. However, the key point in our context is that any and all of this activity is sheeted back to the advice of the trees. The northeast Peruvian Shipibo notion of *plantas con madre* dissolves the nature–culture divide in a way that dramatically transcends the restless dialectic inherent in the term landscape.[2] Access to the evidence for the idea that plants have a mother or spirit that can speak directly to human beings comes for most non-Amazonian people through the ingestion of the psychotropic

compound known as *ayahuasca*. The essential ingredients of this unique potion are the vine and leaves of the chacruna plant, but individual shamans introduce other plant species.[3] The primary reason for ingesting ayahuasca is therapeutic – it acts as a violent purgative. The production of visions, which may inspire storytelling and prophetic scenarios, is considered secondary. Within Shipibo-Konibo societies ayahuasca is not overly fetishized: a wide range of plants, some hallucinogenic, others not, form part of the shaman's pharmacopoeia. However they are encountered and reported, though, the psychotropically induced visions produced in ceremony are remarkably consistent in showing the shaman's patients trees that are cinematically animated and which actively transform, orchestrate and apply the imaginal resources of the jungle to produce archetypal scenarios, whose common theme is the acknowledgement of human descent from the trees. The primary other of non-shamanistic cultures (the animals) is diffused, the originary identification refocused on the vegetal.

This view, internalized in the Lupunaluz group, leads the jungle, or (rain) forest—in western culture the primary locus of the wild—to be interpreted as civilizational. Attributes of density, impenetrability, hostility, even sublimity of affect, are interpreted positively as evidence of a higher order of evolutionary achievement. The jungle's effervescent vitality, its defiance of classification, visualization and even physical access is seen as a critical reproof to the West's intellectual reductionism – reflected in its conceptual, as well as physical clear-felling, of nature and natural complexity. The fact that plants and minds can cooperate (through visions, dreams, and *icaros*) to disclose patterns of organization, inter-specific transformation, and relatedness suggests to the architects and designers associated with the Lupunaluz project a radically different definition of landscape architecture. Inverting the hierarchy that classifies nature as wild, it implies that human beings, orphaned from the Mother Ayahuasca, are the world's wild and disruptive influences.

A similar inversion is implied in the field of design: instead of arranging nature according to human taste (a position that *can* cultivate wildness but which never cedes control), the subject of rearrangement is the individual and collective psyche. It is a mental landscape that needs to be cleared, mapped, and re-oriented. Forty years ago, Canadian ecologist Pierre Dansereau argued, "The need to build a new world is now a necessity, not the utopia that it may have seemed in 1914 or, even in 1939. This is a work of the imagination, and imagination reaches out to hidden dimensions... In other words, the richness of our inscapes is a preliminary to a good management of our landscapes."[4] If this is true, then, according to the Amazonian shaman, the first task is to purge the imagination. Hinted at here is the role creativity has to play in the negotiation of shared ground where human, cultural, and environmental interests are so vastly different. Purging is a form of preparation. It is a clarification of what has been dulled. The author of the term *inscape*, the poet Gerard Manley Hopkins, saw poetry in this light, as "speech purged

of dross,"[5] and as John Robinson argues, although Hopkins's inscape was primarily visual, it could apply to other forms of expression. In an interesting inversion Hopkins characterized the smooth floridness of late-Victorian poetry as "wild", evolving a poetry, which while it might appear sprawling and formless, was governed by "design."[6] The inscape was a landscape purged of dead wood, restored to its expressive potential.

Whatever their origin, *ayahuasca* visions characteristically present kaleidoscopic animations, often with the hyper-real clarity of digital animations. Accepting the symptomatic value of these patterns, Jauregui et al., write, "the healers visualize the energies within the patient in the form of complex polychromatic geometric patterns, and can act on them directly, thanks to the vibrations of the melodies, creating new patterns that help re-establish the balance lost due to illness."[7] Many lines of thought converge on the Lupunaluz project but all of them have as their goal the design of balance: between inner and outer, self and other, humanity and nature. It is recognized that a balance that integrates psychic, physical and social, and biophiliac responsibilities is performative. Legal and ethical frameworks are important but the production of reflective consciousness that the center exists to serve is dynamic. The track into the jungle is not an expedition into the unknown after which one retreats: *vain*, the Shipibo word for track, has the connotation "what is done at the moment."[8] The idea is less to connect than to relate: the primary gesture is not to pull together and bind but to turn one's hands outwards to the forest.

A Shipibo metaphysics of design makes a refreshing contrast with the western approach to, for example, landscape design: the trees dictate or show and, in theory, their patterns are copied and preserved. But how, in practice, is this done? There is not an obvious analogy at the scale of the village between geometric patterns given in dreams and the arrangement of elements. Shipibo villages are fattened tracks, clusters of dwellings that are so strung out that outliers can reattach themselves to other clusters. They are distinguished, though, by the wealth and fertility of their gardens.[9] Beyond this any influence they might have on architects and landscape architects trained in western traditions must be negligible. Around Iquitos, as elsewhere, probably throughout modernizing cultures, the local people aspire to inhabit concrete compounds: they do not share the newcomers' interest in authentic materials. In addition, one needs to differentiate between the practical, everyday reading of the physical environment and the spirit-ridden one of the shaman. It is not clear that a vision was ever meant to be represented. These comments do not invalidate the project but they underline the point that, to respect the reversed intellectual descent line implied by the *plantas con madre* doctrine, it is, and must be, a track in the Shipibo sense: performative, relational, sometimes rather snake-like, or a composition, perhaps, of such energetic paths.

The Lupunaluz group decided to build an energy map of the land. Working from googled aerial views of the land, a dowser in Adelaide (with whom the project architect had previously worked) was asked to map the site's "energy signatures." Skeptics will doubt the value of this; however, whatever the scientific value of the diagram produced, the language in which the dowser explained his reasoning invoked the same principles used by the Shipibo shamanic culture: "The jungle," he said, "is an intelligence matrix that people should experience at least once in a lifetime" and "knowledge is a consciousness of resonances; of the polarization of male and female forces and their balancing. An architect alive to these resonances can be considered an 'intuitive dowser'."[10] Whatever the theory, the scroll-like drawing that emerged from the application of this "lost art" resembled in many ways an intuitive (scientifically informed) site analysis of the kind a landscape architect might produce. A dowser and a landscape architect are probably in accord in wanting to harmonize, to channel, to unblock the field. They both assume the goal of reconnection is good.

The energy map is one of the guides the group used when they began to deepen their knowledge of the land early in 2014. One of the group has undergone shamanic training at the site; the shaman and his wife, resident in the adjoining village, are business partners; and there is a spreading network of intermediaries, local and regional, practical and philanthropic, attracted to the subtle originality of the project. The map acted as a talking point: approximate, its findings occasionally contradicted by the shaman's own energy diagram, it nevertheless offered a provisional orientation to the land. It suggested a differential distribution of energy that could be translated into propitious spots and pathways. Disconnections to be repaired and connections to be respected emerged. In another strand of the project, the group had previously visited the Integatron, an all-wooden dome conceived by George von Tassel as "a resonant tabernacle and energy machine sited on a powerful vortex in the magical Mojave Desert."[11] A key feature of the Integratron's dome is its resonant acoustics. A 60-minute "sound bath" is one of the "signature experiences" offered to visitors. A comparable structure is proposed for the Lupunaluz center – underlining the point that any site survey needs to be conducted on the hypothesis of a reconnection between psycho-physical and geo-magnetic energy centers.

The Lupunaluz project is a work in (rapid) progress. It would be very premature to attempt an overview of landscape design method, let alone a critique of its efficacy. However, its holistic amalgamation of different belief systems in the interest of creating a place of practical spiritual growth is unusual in the attention it gives to design: the parts of the center must fit into the forest – according to principles of resonance whose pattern is intimated by the order of the trees themselves. How this ambition will translate into practical works—conservation programs, therapeutic courses, cultural heritage, and regional development prospects—remains to be seen. But, to judge from the scrupulous concern shown so far to ensure that the process—ideation and materialization—is, as Hopkins would say, all "design," the center will incarnate, or interpret, the

1 Wildness is attributed to neighbors, "The Cashibo are just 'savages' or, at worst, subhuman beasts;" and the world in general is classified oppositionally. "because of the profound dualism of tropical forest mythology in general and Shipibo mythology in particular, there is not one Inca, but two. There is a Good Inca, whom we have already met, and a Bad Inca." Peter Roe, *The Cosmic Zygote: Cosmology in the Amazon Basin* (New Jersey: Rutgers University Press, 1982), 89.

2 Ibid.

3 "The main ingredients in chacruna, for example, are tryptamines which, if taken orally, are rendered inactive by the body's enzymes. The vine, however, contains MAO (monoamine oxidase) inhibitors in the form of harmine compounds, so when the two plants come together they complement each other and a psychoactive compound results which has an identical chemical make-up to the organic tryptamines in our bodies. The mixture, therefore, finds its way easily into our brain, and bonds smoothly to synaptic receptor sites, enabling a powerful visionary experience." Ross Heaven, "Plant Spirit Shamanism: Ayahuasca Medicine," Shaman Portal, http://www. shamanportal.org/article_details.php?id=30 (accessed 29 June 2014).

4 Pierre Dansereau, *Inscape and Landscape* (Toronto: Canadian Broadcasting Corporation, 1973).

Shipibo notion of the track. It will incubate in its communities a heightened reflective consciousness in the form of a more intense relationship with the present.

In this connection I will conclude with a reflection on my own modest experience of the Lupunaluz initiative, which took the form of a site visit and short residency in late 2012. From the point of view of a non-Shipibo approach to landscape design and management, the most familiar element of the stay was walking – guided excursions where the shaman, whose pharmacopoeia was derived from the local forest, introduced us to the trees. Normally, the site visit ahead of the site analysis is immaterial to the design outcome. In the absence of a hosting community, it may even be undertaken alone. The designers come back from their walks, study and arrange their photographs, augment these with scientific data (geological, botanical) and commence a synthetic process of marrying these "site-specific" data to the cultural signature of the site and the functional expectations of the client. But what if the client is a tree? What if the call is to put down roots, cosmically as well as locally? Our guide, by contrast, did not simply navigate a forest: he took us to the source of the design. In other words, our stumbling peripeteia was, if we had the wit to know it, the track in the here and now. It was not a nature ramble; it had the same tense obliquity as a poem by Hopkins. It was the wild as inscape.

More generally, the outsider follows in the footsteps of the guide, but instead of being led to a colonial destination, s/he describes a sacred circuit – the pathways that link communities but also provide the shaman with his access to the forest trees and vines that supply him with his medicines. In other words, access to this "landscape" is inseparable from having (and being) a companion. Initiation is peripatetic and educative. The outsider learns a lexicon of Shipibo plant and animal names, which, later, visit the ayahuasca-taker as spirits. Although it is hard to document (or to generalize), the visions are in a sense dramaturgical: they are, as it were, the energy forms that weave their skein across the rainforest, above and below ground. Around these visions the guided walks implied a landscape design that was essentially the physical expression trace of a psychic domain.

There may be important lessons here for the way we "see" landscape generally. For example, attention to the inscape of an otherwise undistinguished patch of land (typically, an abandoned or overgrown lot earmarked for urban renewal) can disclose surprising lost connections: weeds, clouds, layered decay can in the trancelike introspection of the landscape diviner speak of a lost community of interests. But there is nothing systematic about this. In western landscape design practice, such insights would be considered poetic at best. In the Amazonian context the shamanic intermediary licenses these patterns to appear. The essential insight is that one is never alone. As Hannah Nyala says, "the ties between the tracker and the person up ahead constitute the very heart of tracking. Without fail, following someone else's footsteps always forces me to walk alongside them long enough to rethink the most perverse of my origins. As we track, we too are being tracked."[12]

5 John Robinson, *In Extremity: A Study of Gerard Manley Hopkins* (Cambridge: Cambridge University Press, 1980), 53.

6 Ibid.

7 X. Jauregui, Z.M. Clavo, E.M. Jovel, M. Pardo-de-Santayana, "Plantas con madre: Plants that teach and guide in the shamanic initiation process in the East-Central Peruvian Amazon," *Journal of Ethnopharmacology* 134 (2011): 739–752, 743.

8 See, Sanken Ronin, "Introduction to Shipibo Icaros Language," August 2011, www.anacondacosmica.net/pdf/IntroductiontoShipiboshamaniclanguage.pdf, (accessed 29 June 2014).

9 Roe, *The Cosmic Zygote: Cosmology in the Amazon Basin*, ch. 2.

10 Personal Communication, April 2014.

11 Integatron, "About," http://integratron.com/about/ (accessed 29 June 2014).

12 Hannah Nyala, *Point Last Seen: A Woman Tracker's Story* (Boston: Beacon Press, 1997), 3. See also Paul Carter, *Dark Writing: Geography, Performance, Design* (Honolulu: University of Hawai'ii Press, 2008), ch. 5 for a landscape design project that tried to apply these principles.

MICK ABBOTT
PRACTICES OF THE WILD: A REWILDING OF LANDSCAPE ARCHITECTURE

Mick Abbott is Associate Professor at Lincoln University's School of Landscape Architecture. He is co-editor of a number of books on landscape themes including *Beyond the Scene* (2010), *Making our Place* (2011), and *Wild Heart: The possibility of wilderness in Aotearoa New Zealand* (2011). His recent design research includes projects with Antarctica New Zealand, Air New Zealand, Rio Tinto, Te Rūnanga o Ngāi Tahu, and New Zealand's Department of Conservation. A former outdoor equipment designer, Abbott also completed the first solo traverse of New Zealand's Southern Alps, a journey taking 130 days.

╬ CULTURAL STUDIES, DESIGN, TECHNOLOGY

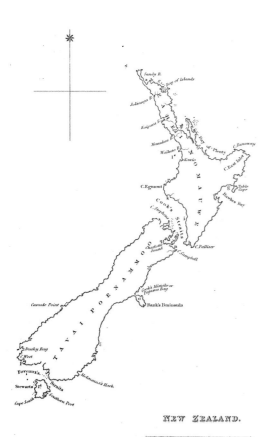

NEW ZEALAND.

The wild, in the discipline of landscape architecture, has been on the outer. John Beardsley frames it as an elitist touristic locale, only available to the wealthy, that leaves the rest of us inhabiting simulations in the mall or "marginal landscapes, salvaging and recycling to survive."[1] James Corner discusses the "sadly sentimental and escapist" qualities of the scenic overview found in national parks: "Here, landscape is nothing more than an empty sign, a dead event, a deeply aestheticized experience that holds neither portent or promise of a future."[2] For Michael Pollan, it functions as an abstract archetype of untouched nature far removed from landscape's key action points found in the "middle landscapes" of the peri-urban.[3]

What is it about the wild–despite the deep landscape-centric dimensions found in its forms, ecologies, meanings, and cultural attachments–that causes landscape architecture to find scant opportunity and appeal in it? This question is especially relevant, given the scale of the world's wilderness areas and their social and commercial value in terms of cultural identity, recreation and tourism, and what is now commonly referred to as ecosystem services.

One reason relates to wilderness's changing meanings. In his pivotal article, *The Trouble with Wilderness – or Getting Back to the Wrong Nature*, William Cronon traces this dynamic quality: from the desolate, godless place of Christ's abandonment, to its incorporation during the 19th century into the sublime, wherein mountains became cathedrals, and a sense of the spiritual was bonded to nature's wonders. This shift, where people were drawn to places they previously abhorred, was born of a change in mind-set, rather than of any physical change: people simply changed the way they let a landscape influence them. Wilderness was thrilling, but more than that, wilderness was the very stuff of which futures were formed: a frontier that, as it rolled back, transformed forests, grasslands, and ranges into pasture, settlement, and wealth. The wild was potent and full of a promise that was based on what Yi-Fu Tuan calls its "generativity."[4]

However, by the 20th century wilderness had been separated out of the economic and cultural creation of nationhood. Instead, it sedimented around an ideal of remote sanctuaries free of change and development: a recreational retreat for increasingly urban lives. Wilderness, while still strong in the imagination, became materially less available. Hence, despite wilderness being routinely understood as a form of landscape, its ideal of being untouched has meant that for landscape architecture, beyond gateway facilities such as visitor centers and hardening high-use trails, there has simply been little opportunity for design.

Instead, wilderness has become the preserve of environmental activists seeking to stem the flow of mining, energy, transport and tourism developments, and disciplines based in management, planning, tourism, and recreation that have examined these tensions. Intellectually it is environmental history, rather than landscape architecture, which has engaged in a sustained discussion of the relevance of the wilderness idea in contemporary relationships with endemic nature.

Cronon questions the "inherent narcissism" of wilderness, in which "we too easily imagine that what we behold is Nature when in fact we see the reflection of our own unexamined longings and desires."[5] He argues that in wilderness we discover a romanticized other, a flawed idea of nature that locates people as separate from it. As such it casts "any use as *ab*-use, and thereby denies us the middle ground in which responsible use and non-use might attain some kind of balanced, sustainable relationship."[6] Cronon's own belief "is that only by exploring this middle ground will we learn ways of imaging a better world for all of us."[7]

The cause of landscape architecture's antipathy to wilderness is, I think, connected to our preoccupation with landscape as a site – as both a pre-given spatially founded locale, and the principal material we design, shape, and physically produce. Dismissed to the background as ephemeral and occasional is the direct design of behaviors, activities, and experiences that enable a landscape "as-it-is" to better shape us.

While much is made of landscape's instrumentality, the value of such instrumentality for landscape architecture remains as a device to increase a site's expressive potential. As such, Corner's call for "the cultivation of landscape as an innovative cultural agent"[8] has been focused on the design of specific sites. Consequently his prescience remains anticipatory: of speaking "here of a landscape architecture that has yet to appear fully, one that is less preoccupied with ameliorative, stylistic, or pictorial concerns and more actively engaged with imaginative, enabling, and diversifying practices – *practices of the wild*."[9] Gary Snyder's eco-philosophy of "the practice of the wild," which Corner echoes, has at its source a performance of wildness: of the path moving from being a formed trail to being *the way* of entering "the relentless complexity of the

world,"[10] in which a place is "spoken" through the manner of our actions.[11]

In contrast, landscape architecture's focus on the site has meant key theoretical developments in the phenomenological generation of landscape are being missed. Anthropologist Tim Ingold articulates a becoming into landscape that is more contingent, temporal, and expansive. Landscape is less a site for form-based expression and more the outcome of our interactions and encounters. As such landscape is open-ended, "never complete: neither built or unbuilt, it is permanently under construction."[12] In this, neither landscapes nor an embodied knowing of them can be pre-configured. Landscape cannot be designed as a precursor to its liveliness. Rather, both the qualities of a landscape and qualities of a person are mutually formed out of "the very activities, of *inhabiting* the land, that both bring places into being and constitute persons as of those places, as local."[13]

This, then, is the critical challenge the wild sets out for landscape architecture. Can we design practices of the wild in which we–people–belong and matter in ways that support endemic systems? And not so much from what we do to a landscape, but rather by what we enable a landscape to do to us.

Contrast, for example, the "being in landscape" revealed through two methods of cooking in the outdoors. In one, a portable gas cooker is taken out of a backpack and placed, along with its adjustable windshield, on the ground. Turning a knob simultaneously releases gas and triggers the ignition; the device is ready for cooking. Such technology might demonstrate excellence in industrial design; however, landscape, in being reduced to a simple backdrop, is made dumb. Landscape loses its particular relevance, and similar experiences become possible whether in wilderness, sitting on your front lawn, or in a store learning to operate the cooker.

The practice of cooking the same food in the same locale, but this time over a portable stove that is fuelled by twigs, creates a landscape that is more instrumental: of walking to a fallen tree to find only half-rotten wood; moving to one side to pick up several hopeful prospects but discarding them as they feel damp (which a simultaneous check of their weight confirms); deciding anything too near the ground in this part of the forest is too wet; seeing a leafless and likely-to-be-dead branch still attached to a nearby tree; of going to break it but finding it

sufficiently supple that it resists snapping; leaving this to find a wonderfully dry, already snapped-off branch hanging in a tree; then continuing in the vicinity to find similar twigs before returning with enough supplies to be able to sort, pack, light, and fan the twig stove.

One technology–the gas cooker–directs landscape to operate as a stage. With the other–the twig cooker–both landscape and person become kinaesthetic, exploratory, tactile, and conversational. In the latter, the unique characteristics and processes of both landscape and person generate a particularity, and with it a richness, of place and identity.

Such a process, as Ingold notes, "has a narrative quality, in the sense that every movement, like every line in a story, grows rhythmically out of the one before and lays the groundwork for the next."[14] The technology of the twig stove choreographs a performance of landscape: as the person is impelled to move about, he or she is enmeshed within the landscape. There are also subtle material differences. In one, remotely extracted and processed fossil fuels from long-buried ancient forests cook the meal. In the other, a localized ethics of acting within living ancient forests, based on intimate decision-making, is foregrounded.

Such an example shows ways in which both people and landscape can be the product of those activities and behaviors that a landscape is enabled to afford. In this, technology is not some transparent or mimetic tool by which the essence of landscape is made available. Rather, as Mike Michaels observes, these technologies are tools that actively interject their own messages to reshape "the affordances of nature by expanding the range of possible actions available to the body."[15] Here, different designs generate different dimensions of landscape.

But importantly the meaning of wilderness is again on the move as it shifts from being a resource-based frontier and solipsistic retreat to being appreciated as an enduring reserve of endemic biodiversity: both interconnected and distributed, as well as microscopic and expansive in scales. The wild is increasingly ecological, and imbued with values associated with biodiversity and resilience – a hotspot where the restoration of threated ecosystems is in contest with invasive pests and predators. In this can be found a significant challenge: how to create innovative behaviors and technologies that foster ecological restoration where people's activities benefit outcomes, rather than adversely impact them.

Here in Aotearoa, New Zealand, fully one-third of the country is public conservation land – tracts of endemic ecosystems larger in size than Denmark and Switzerland together. Examining the social and landscape-centric potential of this

"new wild" is a core question for Lincoln University's Landscope DesignLab. What behaviors create meaningful change in landscapes, and what technologies might then be designed to activate this landscape?

Tim Reed's "Plant-it" mobile app crowd-sources the replanting of forest native species on previously cleared conservation lands. Smartphone applications use GPS capabilities to direct walkers to nearby sites so they can add the mix of plants they are carrying to those previously planted and recorded. This system tunes instructions according to different mobilities, plant species, and quantities people have with them. Here a "practice of the wild" is created from the technology of an algorithm, wrapped up in a mobile app, rather than a preconfigured site-based design. Landscape is performed rather than purveyed.

Also, on the South Island's West Coast, Landscope DesignLab has been experimenting with the role of national parks in the 21st century: intentionally redesigning them from a place made special because of the relative absence of people, to one whose ecological integrity is the direct result of people's actions to volunteer time and resources. At the proposed Punakaiki Living Lab, a mining site is rehabilitated through asking locals and travellers alike to not just look, but also act. Opportunities exist to contribute an hour, day, or week to the work of the nursery (including collecting local seeds, raising seedlings, and potting them out) and to active programs of planting, pest eradication, and citizen science: the goal being to return this rehabilitated site to the adjoining 75,000-acre Paparoa National Park.

The construction of the facility is similarly crowd-sourced by volunteers collecting low-carbon materials including beach gravel, river stones and sands, and fallen totārā timber with which to create gabion baskets, paths, boardwalks, and viewing platforms. It is a project based on an interwoven performance of making, planting, and restoration, that is a response to the materiality and what Ingold calls the "condensed stories" of this landscape.[16]

Such work suggests a shift in the nature of what landscape architecture produces. Rather than the design of a site occurring as a precursor to the practices the interventions afford, the role of the landscape architect expands to include the design of practices from which both landscape and qualities of belonging might be co-produced. Spatial plans become schematic and prospective – a diagrammatic imagination of people's actions. It also suggests—given practices of landscape are also generated by products and devices—an expanded field of operation for landscape architecture, in which a product's functions are designed to draw out behaviors that enable people to "speak" a landscape.

A more proactive and intentional practice of landscape is possible. Yet the question as to what behaviors provide the most benefit to both landscape and people, and then the design of the prompts that could enable such a dialogue, remains very much our "landscopic" frontier. For landscape architecture there is significant scope to expand its generative and creative relationship with landscape beyond the understanding of a landscape's system and the shaping of specific sites. Given landscape architecture's intimate knowledge of the value of landscape, and the ways it enables people and ecology to interact, there are opportunities to design behaviors, tools, technologies, devices, and strategies where endemic biodiversity and ecological resilience are nurtured. This "new wild" demands a design of landscape-centric behaviors in which landscape is produced rather than shaped. Investigating this can also open landscape architecture to the potential of designing innovative actions in other contexts: to foster activities, for example, founded in practices of carbon reduction, waste elimination, water use, mobility, and food production.

And as such, and to paraphrase Thoreau,[17] *a practice of the wild* might yet afford the preservation of a world within which we remain a valued part.

Acknowledgements

Thanks to Professor Jacky Bowring, co-director of Landscope DesignLab, for her active involvement and advice in this research, and to Professors Robert Thayer, Gini Lee, and Simon Swaffield for their very helpful reviews of an earlier, significantly longer, version of this research. Thanks also to New Zealand's Department of Conservation, Professor Nick Dickinson, and the Punakaiki Coastal Restoration Partnership for supporting this research.

1 John Beardsley, "Kiss Nature Goodbye," *Harvard Design Magazine* 10 (2000): 66.

2 James Corner, "Eidetic Operations and New Landscapes," in J. Corner (ed.), *Recovering Landscape: Essays in contemporary landscape architecture* (Sparks, NV: Princeton Architectural Press, 1999), 156.

3 Michael Pollan, "On Design: Beyond wilderness and lawn," *Harvard Design Magazine* 4 (1998): 70.

4 Yi-Fu Tuan, "Foreword," in K. Olwig (ed.), *Landscape, Nature, and the Body Politic: From Britain's renaissance to America's new world* (Madison: University of Wisconsin Press, 2002), xix.

5 William Cronon, "The Trouble with Wilderness; or, Getting Back to the Wrong Nature," in W. Cronon (ed.), *Uncommon Ground* (New York: WW Norton & Company, 1995), 69–70.

6 Ibid., 85.

7 Ibid.

8 James Corner, "Recovering Landscape as a Critical Cultural Practice," in J. Corner (ed.), *Recovering Landscape*, 4.

9 James Corner, "Ecology and Landscape as Agents of Creativity," in G.F. Thompson & F.R. Steiner (eds), *Ecological Design and Planning* (New York: Wiley, 1997), 105 (Corner's emphasis).

10 Gary Snyder, *The Practice of the Wild: Essays* (San Francisco: North Point Press, 1990), 145.

11 Ibid., 115.

12 Tim Ingold, *The Perception of the Environment: Essays on livelihood, dwelling and skill* (New York: Routledge, 2000), 199.

13 Tim Ingold & Terhi Kurttila, "Perceiving the Environment in Finnish Lapland," *Body and Society* 6 No. 3–4 (2000): 185.

14 Tim Ingold, *The Perception of the Environment*, 347.

15 Mike Michael, "These Boots are Made for Walking: Mundane Technology, the Body and Human-Environment Relations," *Body and Society* 6 No. 3–4 (2000): 114.

16 Tim Ingold, "Materials against materiality," *Archaeological Dialogues* 14 No. 1 (2007): 14.

17 Henry David Thoreau's often-quoted "in Wildness is the preservation of the world" is from his 1862 essay, "Walking."

CLAIRE FELLMAN
WATCHING WILD

Claire Fellman is a Director at Snøhetta, an integrated architecture, landscape, and interior design practice based in Oslo and New York. Since joining Snøhetta in 2008, her project work has included the Isabel Bader Centre for Performing Arts at Queens University, the Corredor Central project in Guatemala City, and the Museum for Environmental Sciences in Guadalajara, Mexico. She holds an undergraduate degree in geology and masters degrees in landscape architecture and architecture.

✛ WILDLIFE MANAGEMENT, ARCHITECTURE, CONSERVATION

Adapted to life in post-glacial Europe, and to free movement across the tundra from France northward to Scandinavia, the wild reindeer herds that exist in Norway can be genetically traced to those depicted in the cave paintings at Lascaux. As home to one of the last remaining populations of wild reindeer, Norway is playing a decisive role in the survival of this Pleistocene animal community in contemporary Europe. Now constrained to 23 fragmented patches of mountainous land, the roughly 25,000 modern descendants of these prehistoric reindeer contend daily with the challenges posed by human activity and infrastructure.

One of the larger of these herds lives within the the Dovrefjell-Sundalsfjella National Park and has been defended since 2006 by institutions such as the Norwegian Wild Reindeer Centre and supported by efforts of the Norwegian Defense Estates Agency (Forsvarsbygg), tasked with restoring habitat on former military sites. Using remotely operated robotic excavators to sweep the terrain for unexploded ordnance, and helicopters to apply geologic barriers and soil amendments and at large scale, Forsvarsbygg has undertaken Norway's most ambitious and costly restoration program in the former Hjerkinn firing range, a 165 km2 area contiguous with the national park.

In 2009, Snøhetta was commissioned by the Norwegian Wild Reindeer Centre to design a visitors' center within the former firing range that would raise awareness about the lifecycles of the reindeer and the plant communities on which they thrive.[1] The siting and design of the project required careful choreography of construction activity with the phased erasure of the footprints of human activity on the site. Atop an abandoned mine, Snøhetta designed a car park that is organized in the same manner as traditional reindeer gathering systems found in the region. A series of timber posts form a chute, which guides visitors onto a gravel path leading westward up a valley recently restored with native grasses and other subarctic plantings. The gently sloped path invites visitors to transition from the speed of driving to the pace of walking, and to open their senses to the expansive horizon. Locally quarried slate steps engraved with text punctuate the path periodically, marking out a timeline spanning from 10,000 years BC to the present and offering a window for visitors into the events that have shaped the landscape over time.

The pavilion is situated on the Tverrfjellet ridge, on the footprint of a former military building overlooking the abandoned airstrip and the mountain massif of Dovrefjell to the north. A rusting, raw steel box–welded on site–frames the landscape. The cave-like wooden core, with its integrated benches and soft organic forms, was made using 3D CNC machines and assembled with wooden pegs following traditional boat-building methods. The contrast of the soft organic core with the platonic shape of the steel box is intended to generate both a feeling of being enclosed and safe, and the feeling of being part of the landscape, exposed. It is expected that visitors will carve their names into the wood and leave their marks, creating a sense of ownership and reflecting the intimacy generated between people and place when one is depending on the other.

The Reindeer Pavilion project explores what it means to insert a public space for people within a natural conservation area. In the context of a hazardous site, and an ambitious conservation agenda, a peculiar inversion emerges in which the enclosed space of the pavilion creates a capsule of public space within a territory effectively defined as a private space for nature itself. Designed as a "keyless structure," the pavilion is completely open to the public, with visitors welcome to enter at any time of day or night. The project defines a threshold for people from which they can observe the transformation from military site to what the Norwegian Ministry of the Environment call a "wilderness-like" area [those places which are 5 km or more in a straight line from the nearest infrastructure development].

The full scope of the Hjerkinn PRO reclamation project includes the removal of 90 km of roads, one of its more contested features. Condoned or not, the relaxation of the strict boundaries around the former military site has invited re-colonization of the territory by a variety of users, who participate in knitting the site back into civilian life. In Dovre, these communities include local hunters, mountain bikers, and dog sledders, for whom roads offer a way to enjoy the deeper reaches of a landscape that remains difficult to traverse for many months of the year. Yet these needs are seen to be at odds with protecting the habitually skittish reindeer from the stresses of constant exposure to people.

In Norway, "Allemannsretten", or the freedom to roam, has traditionally protected people's right to traverse both public and private property on foot and to share certain fruits of the commons. As semi-private or semi-public transitional spaces disappear within our cities due to security optimization and surveillance, the public realm is eroded. If our efforts to preserve biodiversity radically constrict the permissible ways for people to engage with the natural environment, it engenders feelings of division between people and animals. Instead, blurred and overlapping boundaries can create a productive gray zone in which the rights of multiple species are actively negotiated, promoting respect, interdependence, and community.

The Norwegian government identifies "wild reindeer" as a term that "does not just refer to the actual animal, but also covers a wide range of ecological and cultural processes that we associate with the species, which was a key resource in European culture for thousands of years."[2] The root word of wilderness in Old English is wilddēoren, meaning wild beast or deer. Perhaps due to their nomadic nature and the scale of their territories, the history and fate of the reindeer are intimately intertwined with our understanding of this contested word.

1 The lead landscape architect for this project was Knut Bjørgum, Snøhetta.

2 Villrein, "Wild Reindeer in 2030?," http://www.villrein.no/wild-reindeer-in-2030/ [accessed 23 June 2014].

NINA-MARIE LISTER
NEW INFRASTRUCTURE FOR LANDSCAPE CONNECTIVITY

Nina-Marie Lister is Associate Professor of Urban and Regional Planning at Ryerson University in Toronto. From 2009–2013, she was Visiting Associate Professor of Landscape Architecture at Harvard University. Trained as an ecologist and environmental planner, she is the founding principal of plandform.com, a creative studio practice exploring the relationship between landscape, ecology, and urbanism. She is co-editor with Chris Reed of *Projective Ecologies* (2014), and author of more than 30 scholarly and professional articles.

ECOLOGY, ENGINEERING, PLANNING, DESIGN

What strategies can design offer to improve landscape connectivity and human and wildlife mobility while reducing fragmentation? If we broaden and invigorate the practice of landscape architecture to consider emerging approaches to transportation planning, there are timely and important opportunities for design to retain, reclaim, and re-establish connectivity. Landscape design offers new tactics–from structures to surfaces–through an emerging class of infrastructures to physically link fragmented landscapes and habitats.

In the last 60 years, the number of cars in the United States has increased more than threefold[1] and settlements have sprawled out from urban centers in unprecedented growth. Yet it's clear that more routes lead to more traffic, and inevitably to further fragmentation.[2] Today, there are more than 4.8 million miles [7.8 million km] of roads on the continent.[3] Americans have one of the highest rates of private automobile ownership on the planet, with more than one-quarter billion vehicles using these roads.[4] Given that commuters now spend on average 1.5 hours per day in the car,[5] it has become disturbingly commonplace and acceptable for wildlife to be killed on America's roads. Collisions between wildlife and vehicles have increased by 50% in the past 15 years. These accidents now cost Americans a staggering $8 billion every year.[6]

But this is not solely a wilderness or rural issue. Those of us living and driving in busy suburban, semi-rural, and urbanizing landscapes are more likely to witness or experience the conflicts first-hand.[7] Growing numbers of wildlife-vehicle collisions with mammals, for example, are leading to higher levels of personal injury and property damage and, with this, rising insurance premiums. While human deaths are not high compared with other accidents, wildlife-vehicle collisions have increased significantly. A recent Federal Highway Administration study[8] reports that there is approximately one to two million collisions between cars and large mammals every year in the United States. This represents a significant danger to human safety and to wildlife populations. Wildlife-vehicle collisions are also increasing as a proportion of the total accidents on the continent's roads.[9] Even if not physically hurt or economically affected by a collision, many people report feeling traumatized after hitting an animal.[10]

Wildlife road mortality is documented as one of the major threats to the survival of 21 federally listed threatened or endangered species in North America.[11] At a much larger scale, conventional road building results in significant losses of habitat for wild animals. Road networks fragment natural landscapes into ever-smaller, disconnected patches in which wildlife must live and move, faced with declining genetic fitness as populations become separated and isolated. Worse yet, wildlife mobility often conflicts with major transportation routes. Most of North America's major highways cross the continent in an east-west orientation, but larger wildlife movement patterns tend to flow north-south following mountain topography, such

as the Rockies, the Appalachians, and the coastal ranges. These landforms have always been important habitat and migration corridors, and they may become more significant. Research on climate change suggests many wildlife species may be forced to migrate in changing patterns in search of new habitats as resources become scarce in their current home ranges.[12]

A current priority for transportation and natural resource agencies is to make highways safer for both drivers and wildlife. One of the proven solutions known to improve safety, reconnect habitats, and restore wildlife movement is the provision of wildlife-crossing infrastructure at key points along transportation corridors.[13] Also known as mitigation structures, wildlife crossings include a range of infrastructures built over and under roadways, which are usually implemented in tandem with warning signs for motorists and exclusionary fencing to force wildlife to cross at the mitigation structures. Deployed correctly and in the right context, wildlife-crossing structures have a near-perfect success rate in preventing roadkill.

Throughout Europe, in Asia, Australia, and in various North American locations, wildlife-crossing structures have been implemented with repeatedly demonstrated success shown in both pre- and post-implementation monitoring studies. Both underpasses and overpasses are growing in use and are constructed in a variety of sizes and designs. Wildlife underpasses are less costly to build and are more commonly used by a wide diversity of species, from interior forest-dwelling species such as black bears and cougars, to smaller species such as reptiles and amphibians, which pose little risk to motorist safety, yet which are often at high-risk for road mortality. Wildlife overpasses are more challenging to implement and more costly, but preferred by certain wide-roaming, larger-bodied and charismatic species-at-risk; such as grizzly bears, elk, bighorn sheep, Canada lynx, and wolverines. Overpass structures are also more widely recognized as they are visible and noteworthy to passing motorists. As such, wildlife overpasses can be designed for greater legibility and often present a timely opportunity for the general public to experience, and identify with, engineered landscape designs that create safer roads while protecting wildlife populations and restoring ecosystem function through improved landscape connectivity.

The best-studied and well-established overpass crossing structures are in Alberta, Canada along the TransCanada highway in Banff National Park. These prototypical structures were not designed exclusively for wildlife; rather, they were modified from conventional transportation-engineered bridge structures using corrugated steel pipe and adapted by back-filling and adding a vegetated surface with approach ramps based on local habitat and landscape type. After a decade of study and demonstrated success, road ecologists[14] are researching new opportunities to evolve the design and function of these prototype structures by asking: could their capacities expand and the cost of their construction contract with a redesign expressly for their purpose? Can collaborations with landscape architecture offer opportunities for improved design solutions? There is also growing interest in using new materials to design lighter, flexible and adaptive infrastructures that may offer effective means to facilitate wildlife mobility and population survival under uncertain climate conditions.

It is increasingly recognized that new design solutions to wildlife-crossing infrastructure are needed. Context-specific designs, using an integrated approach to the engineering and ecology, will tailor each type of crossing–from the substructure to the surface–to particular species, landscape habitats and topography. Site analyses based on monitoring data reveal target species and collision locations or 'roadkill hotspots.' In an era of decreasing public investment in civic infrastructure, there may well be opportunities to reduce costs in some cases by adaptively reusing or retrofitting existing structures for wildlife crossing purposes, whereas new structures may be used to test alternative and emerging sustainable materials at lower lifecycle costs. New solutions to the construction approach and material of crossing structures must also be considered in the context of long-term ecosystem change. Crossing structures may also need to be moved, enlarged or downsized based on changing wildlife movement patterns due to changes in habitats, climate or other factors that become apparent with monitoring over time.

In response to this growing recognition and a need for context-specific integrated design, the ARC International Wildlife Crossing Infrastructure Design Competition was held in 2010 with the goals to raise public and professional awareness and to engage innovative international, interdisciplinary design teams to create the next generation of wildlife-crossing infrastructure for North America's roadways. Since the 2010 competition, the ARC project has grown into an international partnership: ARC Solutions extends beyond a competition for a single wildlife bridge to the broader mission to educate, advocate and innovate for new solutions to wildlife-crossing structures for landscape connectivity.[15] Case precedents from around the world are collected and published, while technical reports, scientific studies and partnership projects are catalogued and highlighted to demonstrate best and next practices.

The ARC project derives its mandate from the understanding that today's transportation challenges are exacerbated by three critical factors: (1) an increasing population and expanding suburban and exurban development; (2) an aging, deficient, and outmoded infrastructure; and (3) a changing climate. From this, the ARC competition challenged five finalist teams to develop solutions that would be cost-efficient, ecologically responsive, safe, flexible, and that could be readily adapted for widespread use in other locations as well as offering flexibility for wildlife mobility under dynamic ecosystem conditions, including climate change. The ARC competitors also faced the unique challenge of designing for two very different clients–humans and wildlife–each with different needs and priorities, yet sharing one problem: the need for safe passage. The design solutions that resulted from the competition are progressive steps in addressing these complex design challenges in the context of road infrastructure for human and wildlife safety and mobility. As part of its mission to educate, advocate and innovate, the ARC project has published and promoted the five finalist teams' concept designs, depicting the material innovations, costs, and various design approaches as a sample of the range of possibilities for a new class of wildlife-crossing infrastructure. In this way, the ARC partnership engages broadly with the public, professionals, and decision-makers alike through research-based education that creatively explores new thinking, new methods, new materials and new solutions for safe passage–inspired by the precedent designs of the competition finalists and disseminating design-based research to state and federal agencies.

1 Bureau of Transportation, *National Transportation Statistics* (Washington, DC: Research and Innovative Technology Administration, U.S. Department of Transportation, 2011) Table 1-11.

2 The problem of habitat fragmentation by roads is well documented in both the scholarly literature and popular media. See, for example: J.P. Beckmann, et al., *Safe Passages: Highways, Wildlife and Habitat Connectivity* (Washington, DC: Island Press, 2010), 396. See also the 2009 documentary film *Division Street* by Eric Bendick: http://www.videoproject.com/divisionstreet.html; and *Bear71*, a 2012 interactive online documentary by Leanne Allison and Jason Mendes: http://bear71.nfb.ca/#/bear71.

3 Central Intelligence Agency, *World FactBook* (2012), https://www.cia.gov/library/publications/the-world-factbook/rankorder/2085rank.html.

4 S.C. Davis, S.W. Diegel & R.G. Boundy, *Transportation Energy Data Book: Edition 30*. (Washington, DC: Office of Energy Efficiency and Renewable Energy, U.S. Department of Energy, 2011) Table 3.5, 3–9.

5 J. Schwartz, "Americans Work 2 Hours Each Day to Pay for their Cars," *The Urban Country*: http://www.theurbancountry.com/2011/05/americans-work-2-hours-each-day-to-pay.html. See also: R. Buehler, "Transport Policies, Automobile Use, and Sustainable Transportation: A Comparison of Germany and the USA," *Journal of Planning Education and Research* 30 (2010): 76–93.

6 M.P. Huijser, J.W. Duffield, A.P. Clevenger, R.J. Ament, & P.T. McGowen, "Cost–Benefit Analyses of Mitigation Measures Aimed at Reducing Collisions with Large Ungulates in the United States and Canada: A decision support tool," *Ecology and Society* 14 No. 2 (2011): 15.

7 Residents of the northeastern states, particularly West Virginia (1:53) and Pennsylvania (1:86), have the highest risk of collision with deer, according to 2011 data collected by State Farm Insurance: http://www.statefarm.com/aboutus/_pressreleases/2011/october/3/us-deer-collisions-fall-map.pdf. In parts of northeastern Canada, particularly Newfoundland, the risk of collision with moose remains an ongoing concern after detection and warning systems have failed: http://www.roads.gov.nl.ca/moose.htm.

8 M.P. Huijser et al., *Wildlife–Vehicle Collision Reduction Study*, Report to Congress, (Washington, DC: U.S. Department of Transportation, Federal Highway Administration, 2007)

9 Beckmann et al., *Safe Passages*, 396.

10 See http://www.highwaywilding.org/.

11 R. Van der Ree, et al., "Effects of Roads and Traffic on Wildlife Populations and Landscape Function," *Ecology and Society* 16 No. 1 (2011): 48.

12 N.E. Heller & E.S. Zavaleta, "Biodiversity Management in the Face of Climate Change: A review of 22 years of recommendations," Biological Conservation 142 (2009), 14–32.

MCS – Modular Crossing System: Balmori Associates

Designed as a modular and efficient "kit of parts," the MCS is a sustainable freeform structure of laminated timber girders, which can be locally manufactured from pine-beetle killed timber, storing more CO_2 than was used in the manufacturing process. The topography of the local landscape is reflected in the underside contours of the structure while the surface habitat, with its wide ramps, is designed to blend seamlessly into the surrounding landscape.

Landshape: Zwarts & Jansma Architects

This scheme proposes a thin-shell, double-curved, concrete pillar-less structure that appears to float across the highway. Using concrete formwork that can be reused for each subsequent crossing, the structure is cost-effective due to the thin layer of concrete required and the intention of repetitive construction. The upper curve of the "landshape" contains the habitat for the crossing, including a system of ponds to serve as a draw for wildlife.

Wild X-ing: The Olin Studio

A double-curved inverted arc, the Wild X-ing structure is a steel and Ductal grid overlaid by a rhomboid micro-grid lattice. The lattice is composed of pre-vegetated lightweight glass-reinforced plastic habitat modules – inserts that can be adapted, replanted, replaced, or expanded as conditions dictate. Customized to local habitat conditions, the modules can be planted off-site and easily transported by flatbed trailer to the site for insertion or replacement.

RED – Research Evolve Design: Janet Rosenberg & Associates

Using lightweight, resilient wood-core fiberglass, the RED structure can be designed in flexible, modular configurations, or "strands" in the landscape, making use of the existing tree canopy as additional habitat between strands. The scheme proposes multiple connections into the site and varied possible routes across the bridge, based on the travel habits and preferences of each target species. The bridge is intended as an iconic structure for humans, signifying the crossing, the landscape and its non-human inhabitants, but is at once unremarkable to wildlife that cannot see the color red.

Hypar-Nature: HNTB with Michael Van Valkenburgh Associates

The structure relies on a modular and cost-effective system of thin-shell pre-cast concrete hypar forms that allow for minimal site disturbance and easy creation, assembly, and deployment, given the availability of local pre-casting facilities. The forms can be readily expanded or adapted as wildlife movements and habitats change, or as site-specific conditions dictate. The scheme is a landscape and structural collaboration, bridging both under and over the road, layering both driver experience and animal preference.

The scheme by HNTB with Michael Van Valkenburgh Associates (MVVA) was unanimously selected as the winner of the 2010 ARC competition. The jury observed that this proposal for a pillar-free, modular structure was at once simple and straightforward, while embodying the complexity and contradictions inherent in the competition brief. In particular, through the use of pre-cast concrete, the HNTB+MVVA scheme makes use of ordinary materials and technology as well as construction techniques that are well established and, notably, accessible in many locations across the continent and therefore has the potential to reduce construction costs. The jury noted in particular that this scheme "marries well a simple elegance with a brute force. It effectively recasts ordinary materials and methods of construction into a potentially transcendent work of design. In this regard it gives us confidence that it could be credibly imagined as a regional infrastructure across the intermountain west."[16]

The winning design, with its repeatable system of modular components made from easily-accessible pre-cast concrete, demonstrates a point of departure for a feasible and effective strategy by which wildlife crossing structures could soon become common in the North American landscape. Yet regardless of the material–recognizing that some diversity in material type and structure is desirable for effective, context-specific designs–it is essential that crossing structures are developed using an integrated design approach and implemented within a network or system of crossings across a landscape type or region. But currently this rarely happens. Projects are still typically perceived as 'one-off' mitigation structures and rarely considered as a part of a holistic mitigation strategy in which a variety of approaches are considered together over a large landscape region. A significant barrier to the widespread adoption of wildlife-crossing infrastructural systems is the institutional planning process itself: the process of commissioning, designing, tendering and building the infrastructure rests almost exclusively within traditional transportation engineering departments. Concept designs are typically initiated by transportation departments as a modification of a conventional structural engineering project with little proactive and specialized consideration given to the habitat design, landscape context and species ecology – considerations that are often a major part of the project cost, and invariably essential to the project's long-term success. Landscape architects and ecologists are not typically included in the design process, and yet post-project monitoring data are clear that the vegetation selection and habitat design for target species are critically important, and that projects may take upwards of three to five years to demonstrate ecological viability and success in terms of landscape connectivity.[17]

Yet as more crossings are built, continuous learning through ongoing monitoring will inevitably improve design efficacy and best practice. Wildlife crossings are already being designed as living experiments, complete with data-gathering technologies built into the structures. In this way, the crossing infrastructures offer rich potential for learning: infrared cameras installed at crossing sites capture and record animals in transit; web cams transmit real-time wildlife movement data to science labs and potentially to classrooms alike; and hand-held applications can bring the data to motorists in a passing car. Based on lessons learned from this monitoring of data, structural designs can and should be adapted to the site conditions and wildlife dynamics with each successive implementation. As such, it is equally conceivable that more prototypical aspects of the other ARC competition finalists' innovations in materiality, technology and ecological approaches will be welcome additions to a promising new typology of infrastructure.

By redesigning the road for two clients–animal and human– wildlife-crossing infrastructure presents a timely opportunity to communicate both the problem and the solution to the public. In this endeavor, landscape architecture has a significant new niche and a potent role in designing safer roads with new infrastructures that are visible and legible, even beautiful. Widespread deployment of this new typology of landscape infrastructure may ultimately change the way we move and live, and with this, reconnect landscapes and habitats through inspired design.

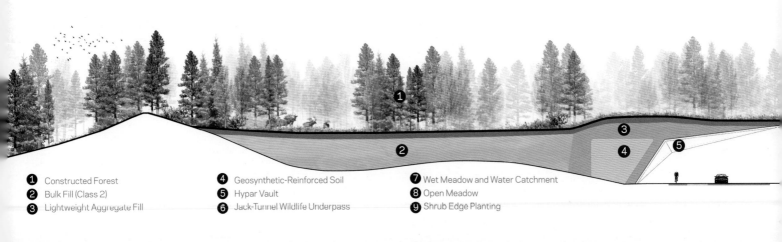

❶ Constructed Forest   ❹ Geosynthetic-Reinforced Soil   ❼ Wet Meadow and Water Catchment

❷ Bulk Fill (Class 2)   ❺ Hypar Vault   ❽ Open Meadow

❸ Lightweight Aggregate Fill   ❻ Jack-Tunnel Wildlife Underpass   ❾ Shrub Edge Planting

1 Exclusionary Fencing
2 Bicycle Path
3 Stormwater Infrastructure Connections
4 Forest, Shrub, and Meadow Planting
5 Hypar Vault Structure Below
6 Jack-Tunnel Wildlife Underpass
7 Wet Meadow and Water Catchment
8 AGS Rail
9 Expanded Vehicular Traffic Lanes
10 Breakdown Lane and Snow Shoulder

Hypar-Nature: HNTB with Michael Van Valkenburgh Associates

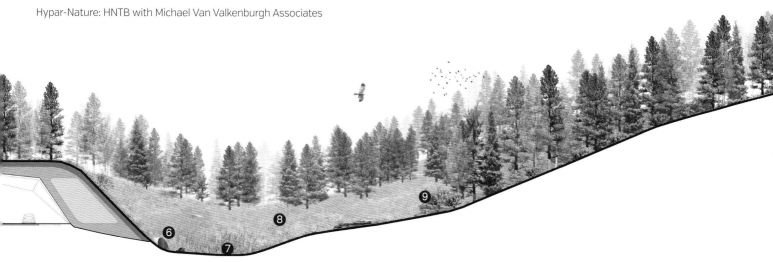

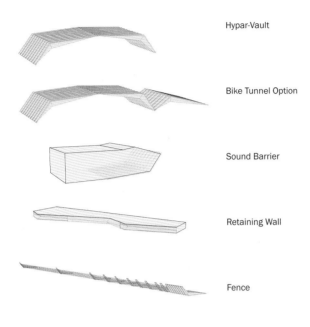

Hypar-Vault

Bike Tunnel Option

Sound Barrier

Retaining Wall

Fence

Construction Method

Meadow

Phase 1	Phase 2	Phase 3
Broadcast annual cover crop	Introduce native perennial grasses	Manage for grasses, forbs, and sedges

Forest

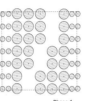 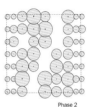 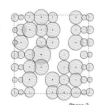

Phase 1	Phase 2	Phase 3
Conifer corridor flanked by aspen	+ 5 years	+ 10 years

Planting Strategy

Acknowledgements The work of ARC Solutions and partners figures prominently in this article. Special thanks are due to the Woodcock Foundation, Dr. Tony Clevenger, and the Western Transportation Institute, and to Ryerson University's Office of Research Services, and to Marta Brocki for image research and assistance.

Selective Thinning

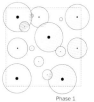 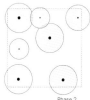 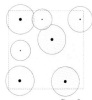

Phase 1

Phase 2

Phase 3

Dense forest with dead standing trees

Selectively thin dead trees/ controlled burn

Seed with native grasses, forbs and sedges

Controlled Burns

 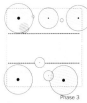

Phase 1

Phase 2

Phase 3

Dense forest with dead standing trees

Selectively thin dead trees/ pile and burn

Seed with native grasses, forbs and sedges

13 A.P. Clevenger & M. P. Huijser, *Wildlife Crossing Structure Handbook: Design and evaluation in North America* [Lakewood, CO: U.S. Federal Highway Administration, 2011].

14 See, for example, the ongoing work of Dr. Tony Clevenger and the Road Ecology Unit at Montana State University's Western Transportation Institute: http://www.westerntransportationinstitute.org/research/roadecology/default.aspx.

15 ARC International Wildlife Crossing Infrastructure Design Competition 2010 [ARC], *Competition Brief*: http://competition.arc-solutions.org/brief.php. For more on the current and ongoing work of the ARC project, see: http://arc-solutions.org.

16 ARC, *Jury Report*: http://competition.arc-solutions.org/jury.php.

17 M.A. Sawaya, S.T. Kalinowski & A.P. Clevenger, "Genetic connectivity for two bear species at wildlife crossing structures in Banff National Park," *Proceedings of the Royal Society of Biology* [February 2014], 281.

Hypar-Nature
HNTE + MVVA Team

EMMA MARRIS
SIMIAN CITY

Emma Marris is a freelance environmental writer. She has a Masters in Science Writing from Johns Hopkins University and worked for many years as a reporter for the journal *Nature*. In 2011, Marris published her first book, *Rambunctious Garden: Saving Nature in a Post-Wild World*. The book highlights alternative conservation strategies that do not focus on holding or returning land to a historical baseline. From managed relocation of species threatened by climate change to the embrace of so-called novel ecosystems, Marris champions a blurring of the lines between nature and people, and conscious and responsible care of our humanized planet.

— ZOOLOGY, CONSERVATION, URBAN STUDIES

Let us spread the joy of conservation and create green urban communities – with adorable monkeys. Cities and dense settlements host 40% of the human population on 7% of the Earth's ice-free surface.[1] That concentration is a good thing; it theoretically leaves more room for the rest of Earth's species. But there's a very good argument for not pushing density to the absolute maximum, for leaving space for plants and animals in cities. The presence of green, diverse undeveloped areas is good for the body, good for the soul, and good for fostering environmental attitudes.[2] Besides, 7% is not nothing. Meaningful conservation can occur here.

Landscaping yards, roofs, medians, and other areas for increased biodiversity is the obvious first step. Planting rare native plants and designing landscapes that can be habitat for rare native animals, from butterflies to small mammals, is an exciting second step. Creating larger, linked habitat areas for rare natives is then the third step. A beautiful pilot project in this vein is Sarah Bergmann's Pollinator Pathway: a mile-long series of parking strips planted with pollinator-friendly plants along Seattle's Columbia Street that links the Seattle University campus to a pocket park called Nora's Woods. Projects that extend beyond a single residence have more impact and, as a bonus, create a community built around a shared conservation objective.

So what might a fourth step look like? What about a community effort to conserve a very rare non-native species? Like maybe a North American neighborhood hosting a population of the highly endangered and absolutely gorgeous Golden Lion Tamarins, native to the Atlantic coastal forest of Brazil?

I got this idea from the National Zoo in Washington, DC. Back when I lived nearby, they had a "free-range" population of the tiny monkeys, each of which is a resplendent reddish-gold and no heavier than a hardback book (or an iPad). The tamarins live in small groups and, according to their handlers at the zoo, "tend to stay within a few hundred feet of their nest."[3] They sleep in tree holes and readily take to nest boxes. They eat bugs and fruit. So all the zoo had to do was put out some fruit for them, tack up a few nest boxes in a forested section of the park and let them go. I remember so well the thrill of walking along the path and seeing their shiny, furry bodies moving just out of reach in the trees. The zoo is situated in Rock Creek Park and, it seemed, there was no particular reason the monkeys couldn't have swung and climbed all the way to Maryland.

With a wildlife biologist on call, some nest boxes, and a community commitment to feed and care for the tamarins, it doesn't seem so farfetched that a city neighborhood could do the same thing. Of course, we wouldn't just want to tip a box of endangered monkeys into a neighborhood without careful thought and preliminary research. Even though the monkeys have very small ranges and are relatively large and noticeable (and presumably therefore somewhat easy to remove should they prove troublesome), there is always the possibility that they could become invasive in their new home – running amok, reproducing out of control, escaping the neighborhood, and threatening local native species. Well meaning introductions have failed dramatically in the past: think cane toads poisoning native Australian animals and the kudzu vine smothering landscapes in the American South. So proceed with the utmost caution, if at all, and with lots of careful monitoring.

But it could be magical. Imagine children waiting for the bus in the morning, watching the grave faces of these orange forest spirits peep out from the laurels. Imagine washing your dishes, staring dreamily at the backyard, and seeing a troop of monkeys clamber over your fence and beeline for the pineapple you put out that morning.

There's no question that the best place for these monkeys would be their evolutionary home, in the Atlantic coastal forest. But there are only about 1,500 of them there and logging has fragmented that ecosystem so thoroughly that there just isn't enough of it joined up right now to support a thriving, genetically rich population. That is why zoos host another 450 – as insurance, as a future source for reintroduction when the habitat improves through the work of conservationist organizations like Saving Species, Save the Golden Lion Tamarin, and Associação Mico-Leão Dourado.[4] Neighborhood tamarin populations could perform the same backup service. They would also enchant, enthrall, build community, and introduce surprise and beauty to our urban lives.

Some conservationists will argue such programs wouldn't be worth the risk of creating an invasive species. I think, for species that biologists believe are at low risk for uncontrolled and harmful expansion and that are highly endangered and in need of backup populations, the risk would be worth it. It would give regular citizens in cities and suburbs a chance to do something truly great, and at the same time to see and enjoy the species they would be supporting, rather than just writing a check to an organization working in distant lands. Doubtless the Golden Lion Tamarin is not the only rare species for which such community-based ex-situ conservation could possibly be appropriate. But it may be the most charming.

1 Erle C. Ellis and Navin Ramankutty, "Putting People in the Map: Anthropogenic biomes of the world," *Frontiers in Ecology and the Environment* 6, no. 8 (2008): 439–47.

2 Judith C.H. Cheng and Martha C. Monroe, "Connection to Nature: Children's Affective Attitude Toward Nature," *Environment and Behavior* 44, no.1 (2012): 31–49; Mat D. Duerden and Peter A. Witt, "The impact of direct and indirect experiences on the development of environmental knowledge, attitudes, and behavior," *Journal of Environmental Psychology* 30, no. 4 (2010) 379–92.

3 http://nationalzoo.si.edu/SCBI/ EndangeredSpecies/GLTProgram/FreeRange/.

4 http://savingspecies.org/projects/past-projects/saving-species-the-golden-lion-tamarin/; http://www.savetheliontamarin.org/ who-we-are/; http://www.micoleao.org.br/.

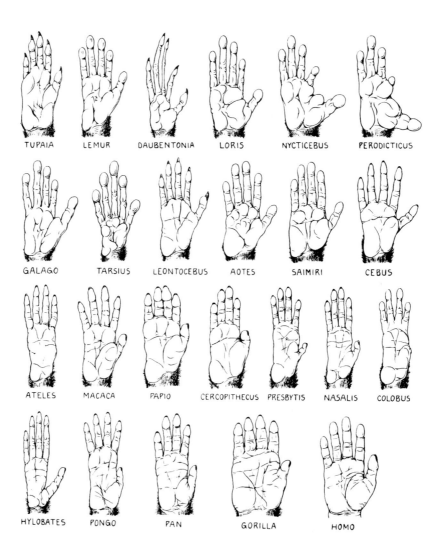

Primate Hands
Adolph Schultz, *The Life of Primates* (Longon: Weidenfeld & Nicholson, 1969).

WDLDMNLT   DTJBKWIRZREZLMQCO   P
Y   YVMQKZPGLXWVHGLAWFVCHQYOPY
MWR   SWTNUXMLCDLEUBXTQHNZVJQF
FU   OVAODVYKDGXDEKYVMOGGS   VT
HZQZDSFZIHIVPHZPETPWVOVPMZGF
GEWRGZRPBCTPGQMCKHFDBGW   ZCCF

Monkey at a Typewriter
Richard Dawkins, *The Blind Watchmaker* (London: Penguin Books, 1991).

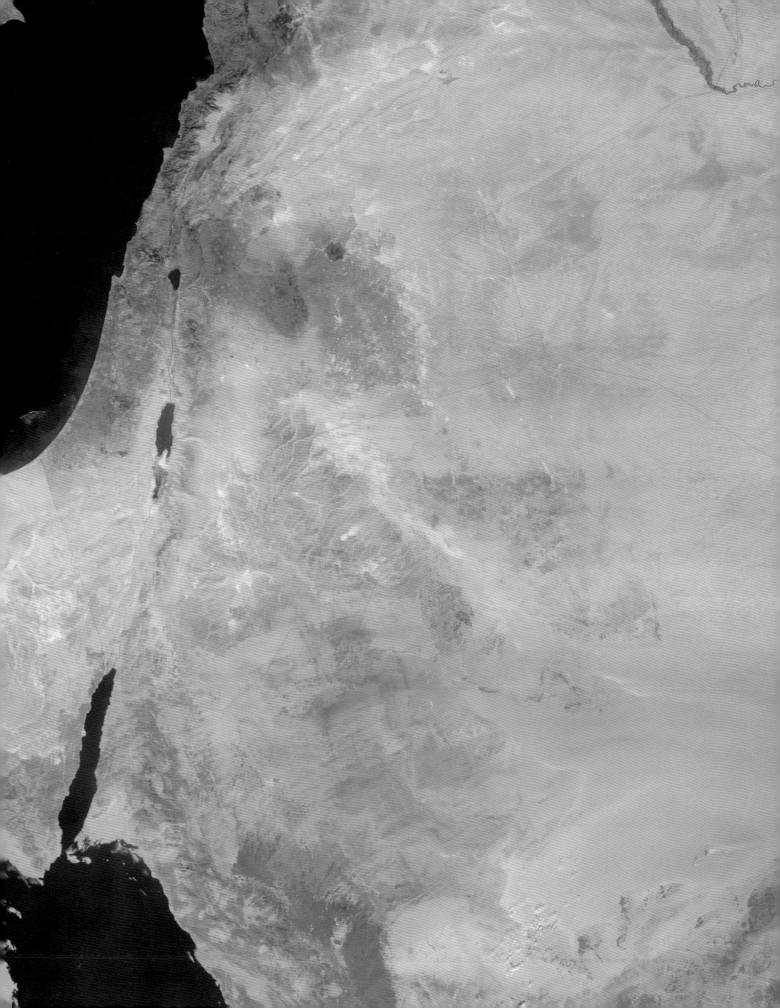

UNIVERSITY OF PENNSYLVANIA SCHOOL OF DESIGN
INTERDISCIPLINARY JOURNAL OF LANDSCAPE ARCHITECTURE

SUBSCRIBE TO LA+ JOURNAL

LA+ Interdisciplinary Journal of Landscape Architecture from the University of Pennsylvania School of Design brings you a rich collection of contemporary thinkers and designers in two lavishly illustrated print issues annually.

Subscriptions start at just $40 a year.

To learn more or to subscribe, follow the links at
WWW.LAPLUSJOURNAL.COM

UPCOMING ISSUES

PLEASURE FALL 2015   TYRANNY SPRING 2015   IDENTITY FALL 2016

www.laplusjournal.com
plus@design.upenn.com

www.oroeditions.com

TIMOTHY MORTON
WHERE THE WILD THINGS ARE

Timothy Morton is Rita Shea Guffey Chair in English at Rice University. He gave the Wellek Lectures in Theory in 201 4. He is author of *Dark Ecology: For a Logic of Future Coexistence* (in press), N*othing: Three Inquiries in Buddhism and Critical Theory* (in press), *Hyperobjects: Philosophy and Ecology after the End of the World* (2013), *Realist Magic: Objects, Ontology, Causality* (2013), *The Ecological Thought* (2010), *Ecology without Nature* (2007), seven other books, and 100 essays on philosophy, ecology, literature, food and music.

+ PHILOSOPHY, ECOLOGY. LITERATURE, CRITICAL THEORY, HISTORY

The term *wild* can frequently mean several things. It can suggest something that is outside of the human (wild animal – as opposed to domesticated) or, less broadly, something outside of human manipulation (weeds growing through cracks in the concrete). This definition of *wild* opposes the human with everything else.

The logistical agricultural project, starting 12,500 years ago in the Fertile Crescent, now covers a huge amount of Earth's surface, and includes, as an extension of its project, industry and computational technology. The violent uptick in its supposedly harmonious periodic cycling—a cycling that influenced Earth systems already is now known as the Anthropocene. What we call Nature (I capitalize it to make it appear for what it is, an artificial construct) is simply the human-created prequel to the Anthropocene. We need to look for wildness outside of Nature.

In effect, this project, which I call *agrilogistics*, is the largest design project ever formed. We are inside it. We eat it. We live in versions of it (suburbia with its neat lawns). We suffer from its unintended feedback loops (the spiraling forced evolution of bacteria and viruses). Agrilogistics is governed by an attempt to smooth over anxiety about the future – anxiety about where one's next meal is coming from. This smoothing over conceals a deeper anxiety concerning the status of beings, which also has to do with the future: not a predictable future, but the radically uncertain *futurality* upon which the predictable future rests. What is a being? What is being? There is a weird openness to things, embodied in the non-agrilogistical idea that things are *tricksters*. Are they alive? Are they sentient? Are they things at all?

These questions are not just relegated to some Paleolithic past – the Paleolithic itself being a concept created by agrilogistics, just as the term *medieval* was created by a later age to denigrate (or romanticize) a time from which one has distinguished oneself decisively. These questions are intrinsic to the reality of things—they are indeed *wild*. And what is significant is that philosophy within agrilogistics, since the later 18th century, has been unable to keep this wildness at bay. Contemporary philosophy—since Hume and Kant, since the inception of the Anthropocene—has been precisely an undermining of rigid thin boundaries between beings. We are reinhabiting the psychic and philosophical space denigrated as *Paleo*, not in the sense of a return to Nature (as in Paleo diet) but in the sense that what is falsely called Paleolithic is in fact more like an *Arche-lithic*, a relation to other beings that has never departed but is only suppressed within agrilogistics, a suppression that results in inevitable ecological, political, and philosophical (not to say psychological) violence.

Agrilogistics itself gave rise to the concept Nature, and so to the concept wild as something outside the human. Nature and wildness, in this respect, are not only dubious intellectual constructs. They are parts of a worldwide, viral war machine whose reproduction, like that of the chair, is debilitating to us and, in the case of agrilogistics, to all life forms. Yet somehow we can't help reproducing it, like polio, YouTube videos, or chairs.

The question whether there really is something *truly* wild–in other words, something not captured within this logistics–is now not only philosophically fascinating, but also politically urgent. The constructivism of the humanities–and the stupid realism that opposes it–arose (since the late 1960s) at exactly the wrong time to address this, which I consider to be the most important question we can ask as we enter an ecological era. Even a global warming denier must now wear sunscreen more frequently.

Is agrilogistics the only show in town? Is nothing wild at all? In this essay I shall argue that there is. And I shall argue it in a way that transcends not only the normative metaphysics of presence that underwrite concepts of Nature, but also nihilist reactions to these concepts.

Why do we think of Nature as opposed to the human? Or underneath it, or beyond it – deep inside me, happening despite me, and so on? It's because a 10,000-year long agricultural project, which began in Mesopotamia and is still in effect, was wildly (pun intended) successful at doing what it implicitly set out to do: establish thin and rigid boundaries between the human and the nonhuman. So successful was this project in the Fertile Crescent that it now covers an awful lot of Earth's non-oceanic space. So successful was it that the vast majority of vertebrate biomass consists either of humans or of their domesticated animals.

These nonhumans include plants such as wheat, which humans adapted to their needs by making the flowers as tiny as possible and the kernels as juicy and easy to harvest as possible. Plants not considered acceptable were defined as "weeds," while insects and vertebrates not considered acceptable were defined as "pests." This thin and rigid distinction cannot hold philosophically, since we know from Darwin that life forms are made up of other life forms and that no clear ontological boundary can be drawn between them in advance. This is also because since Hume (and Kant's underwriting of Hume) it has been illegal to smuggle metaphysical factoids (such as "humans are better than any other life form" or "humans are unique") into philosophy or science. Strangely, though, Kant himself smuggles in such concepts, inheriting a meme that is itself agrilogistical, without question. For instance, Kant only believes that a thing is what mathematics tells you it is – which amounts to a lump of whatever whose "accidental" features are irrelevant. Which goes to show you the scope and reach of agrilogistics. It fouls up even the philosophy that might provide a way to think outside it. This meme that clings on in Kant, like a tick on a stalk of grass or indeed a "weed" growing up through the concrete, is what I call *the Easy Think Substance.*

This is the idea that a thing is a lump of whatever, covered with decorative accidents. There is a strong (metaphysical) difference between this lump and its qualities. Aristotle formalized this substance theory, but it's intrinsic to agrilogistics. I call it Easy Think because it's like the things that are fed into Easy Bake Ovens: some kind of gloop goes in at one end, and comes out cooked at the other, and you pour candy sprinkles on top of it.

Why is the Easy Think Substance intrinsic to agrilogistics, a logistical program that was in effect 10,000 years before Aristotle? Why does the attempt to find wildness outside of agrilogistics, which is to say Nature, always fail? Because the idea that there is a definitive, different outside of agrilogistics *is itself agrilogistical.* The very idea of wildness as outside of agrilogistical space is doomed to fail. Surprisingly, then, it would be best to ignore the rigid, thin divisions intrinsic to agrilogistical functioning, in particular because they never work logically and thus require all kinds of (political, metaphysical, biological, ecological) violence to (pretend to) sustain them. We had better see that quite literally growing between the cracks in agrilogistical theory, let alone agrilogistical practice, are beings not captured by its functioning. We had better find a way to see wildness as *intrinsic* to life forms, and because there is not a thin rigid distinction between life and nonlife (Darwin again), we had best see wildness as intrinsic to *any entity whatsoever.* And this might best be done by seeing wildness as at the heart of what it means to be a thing – wildness, that is, installed at the very heart of being.

In so doing we would be on a firm footing to establishing what wildness might be, since we would now be talking about *ontological,* rather than epistemological, wildness: not wildness beyond our (human) ability to categorize and understand things, but wildness intrinsic to being as such. This would provide sufficient philosophical lift to allow us to think otherwise than agrilogistically. I can't say "outside of agrilogistics" for the very reasons I've just given. So what is required is some kind of judo.

For instance, we could see that the agrilogistical attempt to police its boundaries is an attempt to tamp down contradictoriness. This eventually (again in Aristotle) was formalized as a "law" against contradiction. That this law has never been formally proved, and mostly just taken for granted, tells us a lot already. But there's more: agrilogistics itself, when seen from the vantage point of a sufficient geotemporal scale, is self-contradictory! Let's state that as baldly as we can: agrilogistics attempted to solve a global warming crisis 12,500 years ago, and in so doing brought on even greater global warming. Agrilogistics accelerated in the 18th century–the Agricultural Revolution–and industry grew out of that, whence the steam engine, engine of the Anthropocene, the beginning of carbon emissions sufficient to change geological strata. The very attempt to solve a problem magnified the very same problem!

A host of other problems arose, quite soon too: patriarchy, rigid social hierarchy, what we now call the 1%, drastic health problems, genetic mutations that resulted in shorter, weaker humans. Not to mention the positive feedback loops created by trying to organize and plan on a wide scale: famine, plagues of insects, epidemics (what Greek culture called *miasma*). The Fertile Crescent itself was abandoned relatively soon after the inception of agrilogistics because of desertification, thus giving rise to the long history of "civilization," spreading west. Wash, rinse, repeat...the Dustbowl in 1920s America. Wash, rinse, repeat...an area of the Amazon rainforest the size of Wales depleted each year to farm cattle. Wash, rinse, repeat...the Sixth Mass Extinction Event in the 4.5 billion-year history of life on Earth, caused by global warming caused by humans.

If we like this situation–which has turned out to be a most efficient way of ridding Earth of many of its life forms–then we had better keep cleaving to the law of non-contradiction, and the Easy Think Substance that is its consequence, both hardwired into social space. Here is the field, I can plow it, sow it, leave it fallow, farm livestock – but there it remains, uncomplicatedly itself, no matter what accidents I decorate it with. In other words, cleaving to the (unproven) law and its Easy Think Substance results in a metaphysics of presence that has been disastrously violent in every domain (social, psychic, philosophical). Since science and math do not cleave to this metaphysics (just ask Darwin or a quantum physicist or the mathematician Gödel), why are we still keeping it up?

Since this upkeep of non-contradiction is politically and ecologically (same thing) dicey to say the least, why not admit that in some cases things can be perfectly logical *and* contradict themselves? In other words, there is no need to seek an a-logical "wild" outside of thought, outside of reason. It might be *more reasonable* to let things be wild.

To be truly wild, a thing would have to contradict itself *in order to be itself*. A thing would have not to be metaphysically present, not even to itself. Appearance (what Easy Think theory calls *accidents*) must be inseparably glued to what a thing is (what Easy Think theory calls *substance*) such that there is, 1) no difference between them, and 2) a profound and irreducible gap between them: ontological wildness, not just epistemological. Or rather, a thing, in order to be a thing, would be caught in its own weird hermeneutical loop or spiral, without the need for some (human) subject or observer or measurer or measuring device–or Geist, or history or (human) economic relations or some other kind of human presence– to cause this loop. Without, in other words, any of the substitutes for what is called *naïve* metaphysics by so-called sophisticated correlationist thought, itself metaphysical insofar as it posits not some underlying substance but an overlying (human) evaluator that gets to pry open the thing to find out whether the light is on inside its refrigerator.

We can get to this wildness by considering a logical system. A logical system, in order to be true on its own terms (coherent), *must be able to talk nonsense*; that is, it must be *wild at heart*

just to exist at all. It must–Russell and Whitehead's *Principia Mathematica* notwithstanding–be able to make sentences such as "This sentence cannot be proved," maddening, Trickster-like, loopy sentences, self-referential like the self-swallowing serpent, the Ouroboros.

Logic, before it is logistics, is a kind of *gathering* of things, as in "I gather that you are feeling unwell today." A collecting or recollecting. So if logical systems must be inconsistent in order to be coherent, so must pencils, Neanderthals, trickles of water in a desert, Sirius, and baskets of fruit. *To exist is to be wild*. This is easy to demonstrate empirically, since the attempt to smooth out and cover up this wildness has resulted in the 12,500-year loop that denies it's a loop, the avoidance of anxiety that has resulted in a greater anxiety, the avoidance of global warming that has resulted in greater global warming, the washing of hands with antibacterial soap that has resulted in more threatening bacteria, the pesticides that have resulted in bee death, which in the end will result in agricultural failure.

Wild in this deep ontological sense means *a thing is a thing because it is in a loop with itself, such that it is impossible to tell where its appearance stops and its essence starts, though appearance and essence are different*. Humans have been blocking this fact for twelve-and-a-half-thousand years, which is why it sounds so counterintuitive. But we now need to think this fact, because we are operating on a scale sufficient deeply to influence Earth at a geological level, and therefore on all the levels above that.

Planning and designing on a planetary scale–that is, on a scale in which there is no "away," no background and therefore no (inevitably anthropocentric) "world," a scale that is fully ecological–means allowing things to be wild. The attempt to plan for the next meal or the next month or the next five years looks coherent on a small scale, an anthropocentric one, if we ignore the consequences, the loops. And the attempt to limit the loopiness of beings and of being that underlies more mundane anxieties also results in drastic (and related) problems. But just as Euclidean space is no way to describe a very large thing–you need Gaussian, curved, space for that–in the same way you need to allow for loops and weird twisted things (a tautology, since *weird* means *twisted*) if you are going to plan on a global warming scale, namely a 100,000-year one.

Designing on a planetary scale means not covering Earth, or relations between beings on Earth– such as political relations–with a one-size-fits-all umbrella. There is a certain return to a Lyotardian poststructuralism in this thought. But it is no longer an epistemological poststructuralism. Rather it is an ontological one, and therefore it is truly post-modern, rather than postmodern.

1

2

3

This Is Not Here

4

5

From: LA+
To: Tim Morton
Subject: WHERE THE WILD THINGS ARE
*Tim, we are exploring image options for your article.
Do you have any ideas? Go wild!*

From: Tim Morton
To: LA+
Subject: Re: WHERE THE WILD THINGS ARE
Excellent! Okay:
1. *An ear of wheat*
2. *A footprint on the moon*
3. *A rusty nail*
4. *Yoko Ono's "This is Not Here" (if permission allows)*
5. *The eye of a mallard.*

TIMOTHY A. MOUSSEAU + ANDERS P. MØLLER
LANDSCAPE-SCALE CONSEQUENCES OF NUCLEAR DISASTERS

Timothy A. Mousseau is a Professor of Biological Sciences at the University of South Carolina. His research is concerned with the ecology and evolution of animals and plants with a special interest in how adaptations to changing environments evolve in natural populations. Mousseau has studied the impacts of radioactive fallout from the Chernobyl and Fukushima disasters on natural populations of birds, insects, plants, and microbes. He is a Fellow of the American Association for the Advancement of Science, a Fellow National of the Explorers Club, and a member of the Cosmos Club (Washington, DC).

Anders P. Møller is an evolutionary biologist and Research Director at the National Center for Scientific Research, at the Université Paris-Sud, France. He has published more than 700 scientific papers that have been cited more than 40,000 times. Møller's current research includes the ecological and evolutionary consequences of urbanization and climate change on birds. He has conducted research on the biological effects of low-dose radiation at Chernobyl since 1991 and at Fukushima since 2011.

+ EVOLUTIONARY BIOLOGY, GENETICS, ECOLOGY

Disasters such as those that occurred in Chernobyl in 1986 and Fukushima in 2011 have been largely overlooked from the large-scale landscape perspective because radiation evades our senses and can only be detected using electronic devices. However, the direct consequences of radiation on biochemicals (e.g., DNA) can have considerable and cascading impacts on individuals, populations, communities, and broader ecosystems.

The nuclear accidents at both Chernobyl and Fukushima released enormous quantities of radioactive elements that were dispersed by the prevailing weather at landscape scales with land areas of approximately 200,000 km2 and 15,000 km2 significantly contaminated in these regions, respectively. The radioactive materials were not uniformly dispersed and created a mosaic of "hot" and "cold" microhabitats scattered across these regions. This radioactive patchwork has provided a unique opportunity to investigate the genetic, ecological, and evolutionary impacts on biological systems with a degree of replication, and hence scientific rigor, not possible using laboratory or traditional field studies, which are often constrained to a limited and rather unnatural range environmental heterogeneity. It is expected that the interactions between natural environmental factors and radioactive contaminants likely play a large and significant role in determining ecological outcomes of these disasters and thus it is imperative that studies of radiation effects be conducted in nature, at a landscape scale.

Despite the unprecedented magnitude of these disasters, there have been many reports in the popular media and regulatory agency literature of limited health and environmental impacts stemming from the radiological aspects of the Chernobyl and Fukushima disasters. In fact, the Chernobyl Forum's 2006 report suggested that plants and animals had thrived since the disaster:

> The recovery of affected biota in the exclusion zone has been facilitated by the removal of human activities...As a result, populations of many plants and animals have eventually expanded, and the present environmental conditions have had a positive impact on the biota in the Exclusion Zone. Indeed, the Exclusion Zone has paradoxically become a unique sanctuary for biodiversity.[1]

The more recent report of the United Nations Scientific Committee on the Effects of Atomic Radiation (UNSCEAR) also suggested that impacts to non-human biota beyond the

areas of highest contamination would be "insignificant."[2] However, these claims were made largely in the absence of supporting data. In direct response to these claims, our research team has made more than 30 expeditions to Chernobyl and 10 to Fukushima and has published more than 60 peer-reviewed papers documenting the biological impacts of these disasters.[3]

Among the most notable observations made early in our studies were the large numbers of generally intact Scots Pine (*Pinus sylvestris*) tree trunks scattered haphazardly across many of the more highly contaminated regions of the Chernobyl Exclusion Zone. These trees were killed by the high doses of radiation that accompanied the initial explosion and in many areas the trees have never returned because of the high radiation levels that persist in these areas. In addition to the tree trunks, we also observed thick layers of leaf litter on the forest floor. Inspired by these observations, in 2008 we conducted a large-scale experiment where we placed more than 600 bags of leaf litter across the Zone to test the hypothesis that decomposition processes were being disrupted by the radioactive contaminants, thus leading to the accumulation of dead plant material on the ground.

The results from this experiment were conclusive: in areas of high radiation, decomposition was 50% slower than in clean areas, with variation in microbial activity (rather than insects or other invertebrates) the leading cause of decline in decomposition activity.[4] It seems likely that these effects on microbial activity are also one cause of the decreased productivity observed for several tree species.[5] The direct effects of radiation on tree growth can be easily seen from measurements of tree ring growth increments and qualitative changes in wood color and density. In addition, in many areas of the Zone, the normally tall and straight Scots Pines are twisted and deformed as a result of the direct toxicity and mutagenic impacts of the radioactive contaminants on their apical meristems. Although deformities in tree architecture can be caused by many factors, the prevalence of such malformations in areas of high radiation has been repeatedly documented leaving little doubt concerning the dominant cause in the Chernobyl region. To date no similar studies have been conducted in Fukushima, although anecdotal observations of high branch fall from Japanese cedars (*Cryptomeria japonica*) in areas of high radiation are highly suggestive that the forests of this region may have been affected in similar ways.

Abnormal development related to the radiation can also be seen in many other organisms. The first directly observed abnormalities were patches of white feathers in bird plumage that are much more common in areas of high contamination.[6] The appearance of these partial albinos is believed to reflect the direct effects of ionizing radiation on the specialized cells (melanocytes) that produce pigments in feathers and skin, and indirect effects of radiation on the availability of key intracellular antioxidants (e.g. carotenoids and glutathione). These antioxidants serve the dual role of quenching the reactive oxygen species (ROS) that are generated by ionizing radiation as well as precursors to the pigments found in many organisms. If antioxidants are used for coloration, they cannot be used as a defense against ionizing radiation, and the ability to adjust this trade-off may be an important factor related to adaptation to radiation that has been recently reported for some birds in Chernobyl.[7]

We have also documented many other effects of radiation including increased rates of cataracts and tumors on the heads, bodies, and feet of birds. Some insects also show large and obvious effects of radiation on color patterns on their exoskeletons. For example, the "facemask" patterns on the firebugs of the region show dramatic aberrations and asymmetry in form in many individuals living in radioactive areas.[8] Recent studies of butterflies in Japan show similar morphological consequences of the genetic mutations resulting from exposure to radiation.[9]

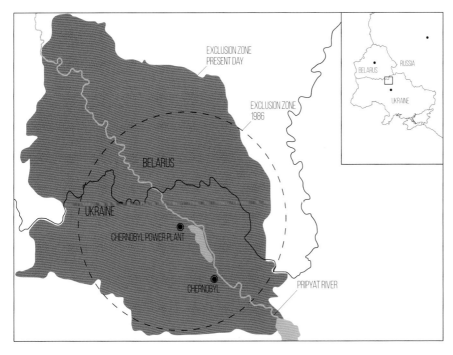

Above: Cross sections through frozen Scots Pine reveal changes in wood color, quality, and growth rate following the Chernoybl disaster.

Left: Chernobyl Exclusion Zone in 1986 and at present day.

It is becoming increasingly clear that the effects observed for individuals have a cascading influence on the biological community and ecosystem as a whole. Over the course of 2006–2008 in Chernobyl (Ukraine and Belarus) and 2011–2013 in Fukushima, a total of 896 and 1,100 surveys of animal distribution and abundance were conducted at each location, respectively. We called this a *massively replicated biotic inventory* experiment. The objective was to determine, with a high degree of confidence, the impacts of radiation on productivity and biodiversity in these regions. The statistical analyses that are possible by use of a large landscape approach permits the investigation of radiation effects independently of other environmental factors known to influence animal abundance, and has the added important advantage of not requiring baseline information from prior to the disasters. The overriding message from these studies was that most birds, insects, spiders and mammals showed significant declines in health and population in areas of high radiation in the Chernobyl regions following 20+ years and a similar number of generations.[10] In Fukushima, following just four months of exposure, birds, butterflies, and cicadas showed declines, while many other groups appear not to have been affected (although mammals have not yet been surveyed).[11] The approach we have taken provides a very sensitive and robust analysis for radiation effects while controlling for the possible contributing effects of human habitation and local micro-environmental factors.

In sum, these findings clearly demonstrate landscape-scale individual, population, and ecosystem consequences of these nuclear disasters, with many examples of developmental abnormalities and deformities that likely contribute to the depressed abundances and biodiversity seen in radioactive parts of the Chernobyl and Fukushima regions. These findings contrast starkly with the optimistic unsupported claims made by the United Nations Chernobyl Forum and UNSCEAR committees. Continued study will be required to determine not only the time-course for population and community adaptation to this perturbation, but also if (and when) these regions will ever again be suitable for human habitation.

1 Chernobyl Forum, *Chernobyl's Legacy: Health, environmental and socio-economic impacts* (Austria: International Atomic Energy Agency, 2006) 30.

2 United Nations Scientific Committee on the Effects of Atomic Radiation, "UNSCEAR 2013 Report to the General Assembly with Scientific Annexes" (New York: United Nations, Vol. 1, 2014) 11.

3 Most of these publications are available at http://cricket.biol.sc.edu.

4 Mousseau, T.A., G. Milinevsky, J. Kenney-Hunt, A.P. Møller, "Highly Reduced Mass Loss Rates and Increased Litter Layer in Radioactively Contaminated Areas," *Oecologia* (2014), doi:10.1007/s00442-014-2908-8.

5 Mousseau, T.A., S.M. Welch, I. Chizhevsky, O. Bondarenko, G. Milinevsky, D. Tedeschi, A. Bonisoli-Alquati & Møller, A.P., "Tree Rings Reveal Extent of Exposure to Radiation in Scots Pine, Pinus Sylvestris," *Trees – Structure and Function* (2013), doi: 10.1007/s00468-013-0891-z; Møller, A.P., F. Barnier & T.A. Mousseau, "Ecosystem effects 25 years after Chernobyl: pollinators, fruit set, and recruitment," *Oecologia* (2012), doi:10.1007/s00442-012-2374-0.

6 Møller, A. P. & T. A. Mousseau, "Albinism and Phenotype of Barn Swallows Hirundo rustica from Chernobyl," Evolution, 55 (10) (2001): 2097-2104; Møller, A.P., A. Bonisoli-Alquati, and T.A. Mousseau, "High Frequencies of Albinism and Tumors in Free-living Birds at Chernobyl," *Mutation Research* 757 (2013): 52–59.

7 Galvan, I., A. Bonisoli-Alquati, S. Jenkinson, G. Ghanem, K. Wakamatsu, T.A. Mousseau, A.P. Møller, "Chronic Exposure to Low-dose Radiation at Chernobyl Favors Adaptation to Oxidative Stress in Birds," *Functional Ecology* (2014), doi:10.1111/1365-2435.12283.

8 Thompson, H, "Chernobyl's Bugs: The art and science of life after nuclear fallout" (April 14, 2014) http://www.smithsonianmag.com/arts-culture/chernobyls-bugs-art-and-science-life-after-nuclear-fallout-180951231/?no-ist (accessed 16 June 2014).

9 Hiyama, A., Nohara, C., Kinjo, S., Taira, W., Gima, S., Tanahara, A., Otaki, J.M, "The Biological Impacts of the Fukushima Nuclear Accident on the Pale Grass Blue Butterfly," *Scientific Reports* 2 (2012): 570, doi:10.1038/srep00570.

10 Møller, A.P. & T.A. Mousseau, "Efficiency of Bio-indicators for Low-level Radiation under Field Conditions," *Ecological Indicators* 11, no. 2 (2011): 424-430, doi:10.1016.j.ecolind.2010.06.013. See http://cricket.biol.sc.edu for access to other papers detailing these studies.

11 Møller, A.P., A. Hagiwara, S. Matsui, S. Kasahara, K. Kawatsu, I. Nishiumi, H. Suzuki, K. Ueda, and T.A. Mousseau, "Abundance of Birds in Fukushima as Judged from Chernobyl," *Environmental Pollution* 164 (2012): 36–39; Møller, A.P., I. Nishiumi, H. Suzuki, K. Ueda, and T.A. Mousseau, "Differences in Effects of Radiation on Abundance of Animals in Fukushima and Chernobyl," *Ecological Indicators* 14 (2013): 75–81.

Opposite: Chernobyl birds - deformities, albinism, and tumors.

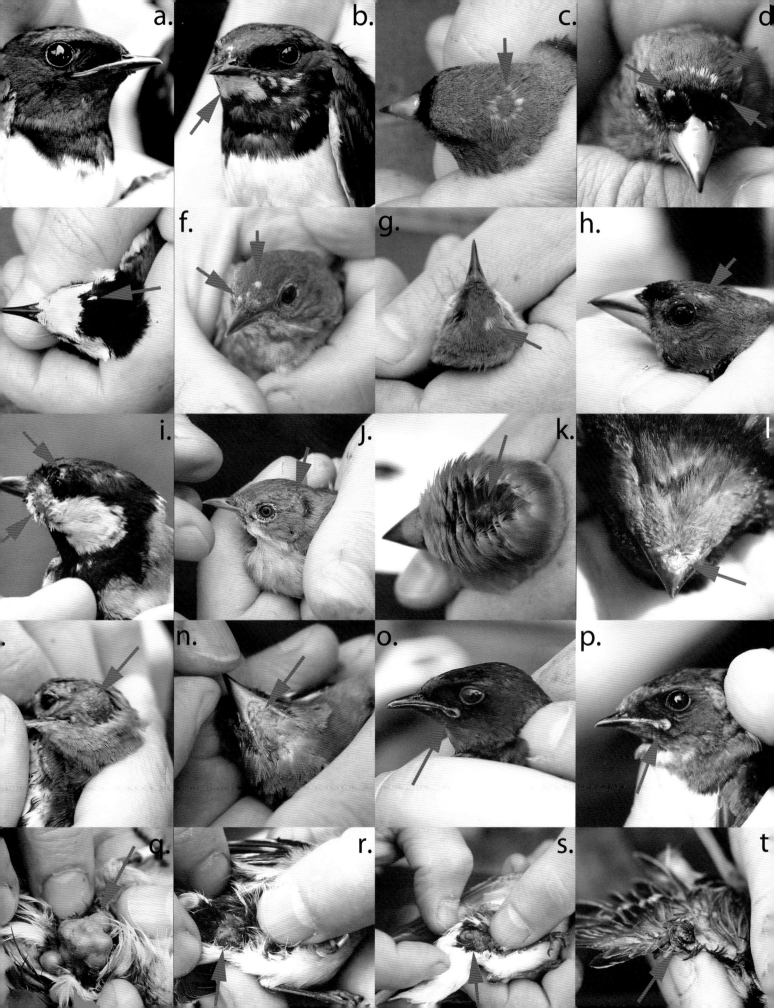

ORKAN TELHAN
THE TASTE OF THE NEW WILD

Orkan Telhan is an interdisciplinary artist, designer, and researcher whose investigations focus on the design of interrogative objects, interfaces, and media, engaging with critical issues in social, cultural, and environmental responsibility. Telhan is Assistant Professor of Fine Arts (Emerging Design Practices) at the University of Pennsylvania. He holds a PhD in Design and Computation from MIT and his individual and collaborative work has been widely exhibited, including at the 13th Istanbul Biennial, the Architectural League (New York City), Archilab, and the New Museum of Contemporary Art (New York City).

+ GENETICS, AGRICULTURE, BIOLOGY

Contemporary biotechnologies are continuously reimagining the "wild." Organic and inorganic matter—the raw materials of life—are reinterpreted every day to become better, cheaper, and more resilient products. From genetically modified produce to designed ecologies, our relationship with what we used to consider wild gets revised with respect to our expectations of the living. Landscape and habitats are transformed in favor of plants that provide higher profit margins than native wilds. Meat, grown in laboratories, promises synthetic analogs for emerging protein markets to enable us to enjoy the taste of wild without the emotional burden of killing animals. The human body, once again, is turning into a wild territory, attracting researchers from life sciences and design fields to develop ways to colonize the newly discovered microbial landscapes that lie within. In this essay, I explore these three "new wilds" and discuss how the wild is increasingly becoming a design space, demanding new cultural references and codes to reflect today's socio-political and economical desires.

Nature "as is" is now competing with better (and wilder) alternatives. Better in the sense of being more resilient and more sustainable, but also potentially wilder with even more of the diverse and unpredictable features that are historically associated with untouched natures. Newly imagined wilds promise ways to save the wilds of the past. Sandalwood, the genus known as *Santalum*, is one of the most valuable plants in the world. The exotic sweet sandalwood oil, which is the most precious part of the plant, has numerous applications in the fragrance, cosmetics, and pharmaceutical industries. The cost of pure wild Indian sandalwood oil can run to US$1,900/kg, making the plant a highly valuable commodity in international trade. Such demand makes sandalwood an overharvested plant; the conservation of certain wild species of sandalwood is highly regulated around the world and most commercial production has shifted towards domesticated plants grown on farmlands and plantations.

Given its precious and precarious nature, sandalwood oil has been under scrutiny for some time as a candidate for biosynthesis: synthesizing parts of the oil by transferring its genes to microbial organisms and growing the desired constituents in industrial fermenters. If biosynthetic oil can supply a significant amount of the demand, it can potentially reduce the stress on the wild and protected sandalwood species. While factory-grown oil is not as authentic as the wild oil derived from the nature-born tree, the synthetic bacterial oil can still maintain the growing demands from the fragrance and cosmetics industries to keep sandalwood farmers in business and save both the wild and the plantation-grown species from total extinction. Ultimately, both the authentic wilds and their substitutes rely on matters of perception to claim credibility and market share.

Opposite: Sandalwood plantation, Western Australia.

New scopic regimes can also render once-domesticated landscapes into new wilds. The human body—which is drawn page after page in anatomy atlases and visualized slice after slice in fMRI archives—now poses a new territory, a new unknown. The quest for mapping the microbial landscape of the body—known as the human microbiome project—tells us that we host 10 times more foreign organisms in our bodies than our own cells; anywhere from our skin to our ear channels. The body comes back as the new wilderness – an uncharted landscape that demands alternative visualizations to map out actually which foreign organism is living with us: when and where.

As this new landscape is revealed before our eyes, so too are initiatives for re-domesticating the body with predictable, personalized, and specially enhanced microbial species. Companies like uBiome and American Gut already offer human feces analysis with advanced gene-sequencing techniques that can provide a total analysis of the personal microbiome from a swab – akin to drug or pregnancy tests. Without breaking it down to individual genus and species, shotgun sequencing can measure the DNA content of the entire cartography of the feces and provide higher resolution information about what might be possibly hosted there. While traditional methods of gene analysis rely on the ability to sequence what we can culture in lab environments, next-generation sequencing allows ways to analyze genetic material without associating them with known species and therefore yield the potential of discovering unknown organisms. Between different interpretations of signal and noise now lies a new data-driven wilderness that does not confine to the limits of ocular regimes and allows us to render new territories negotiated between the cells and foreign organisms.

Newly designed wilds also put new faces to our changing tastes and desires. With increasing concerns about reliability of meat production due to global warming and the inhumane treatment of food animals, lab-grown meat is increasingly claiming its niche within gastronomic practices. It marks one of the latest stages in our transition from hunter–gatherers to industrial meat producers who are willing to leave the animal behind and culture the meat *in vitro*: outside a living body. Being backed by entrepreneurs such as Google co-founder Sergey Brin, a number of commercial ventures (e.g., Modern Meadow) are working on ways to advance victimless meat production and make it a viable commercial reality for the growing protein market in developing economies.

In addition to being very costly and time consuming, the synthetic meat hype also comes with a major caveat. The lab-grown meat depends on an animal product known as Fetal Bovine Serum (FBS), which provides the vitamins, amino acids, and other nutritious media needed by the animal cells to grow. Living still depends on other living after all. While becoming the new wild off the laboratory bench, synthetic meat inevitably attracts research towards making synthetic FBS, which promises to make the meat even more artificial in the process of making it entirely nature-free. Lab-grown meat will ultimately offer different degrees of wildness based on its natural ingredients and will open itself to matters of preference and taste. Those who cannot pay the premium price for nature-free meat will have to settle for the cheaper—and, paradoxically, wilder—version of the synthetic.

Like all narratives, the wild will continue its synthetic turn and will acquire new styles, tastes, and public images. Along with nature-free sandalwood scent, groomed gut floras and lab-grown burgers, the synthetic wilds will be ready to respond both to consumer desire and to conservationists' interpretation of the ecological crisis. There will also be plenty of wildernesses that will inevitably have to go wilder to have a chance to survive against the synthetic.

Above: Three pieces of *in vitro* meat grown at Biofilia, Helsinki.

Opposite: Skin bacteria grown by artist Sonja Bäumel in a body print made on agar.

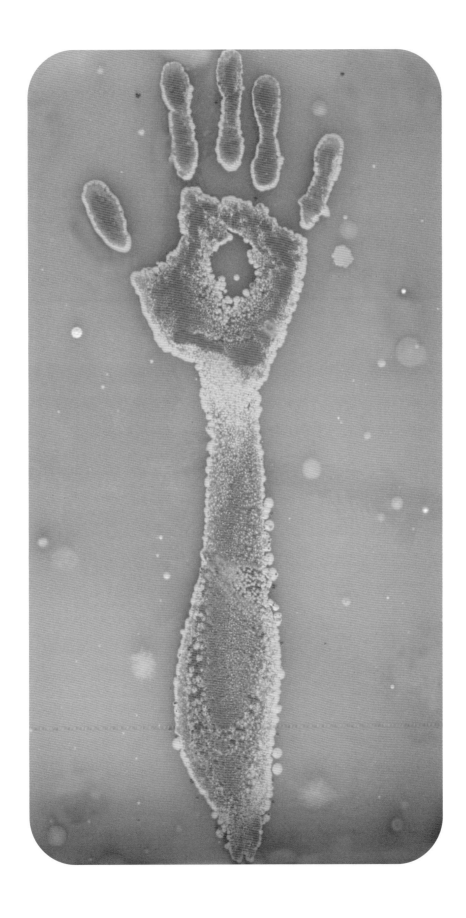

In the project *Expanded Self*, Sonja Bäumel has used her own body to explore bacteria from an aesthetic point of view, which at the same time is an attempt to challenge our perception of the human skin and who we are. Supported by bacteriologist Erich Schopf, Bäumel has found a unique way of visualizing the invisible surface of the human body. She uses a gigantic petri dish as canvas and the bacteria living on her own body as color.

After the application of the invisible bacteria colors, the body is imprinted on agar – the nutritive substance for bacteria. After a few days, a living landscape begins to grow. It consists of a unique mixture of the bacterial life that existed on the artist's body on a certain day, in a certain place. Explaining her motivation, Bäumel says:

> I am interested in outlining a 'bigger picture' and particularly in understanding in which way we, humans, are connected to our surroundings and enveloped in an unknown network, which could perhaps lead us to identify new forms of possible interaction between us and the environment.

This imprint of a human body is a kind of metaphor for new points of view of our identity. If we merge the genetic material of all our body's inhabitants it comprises 10 times more information than our own DNA. We are only just beginning to understand how this astonishing community of different life forms works on us. Our body does not end with our skin: it extends into the landscape in an invisible way.

Sonja Bäumel is an interdisciplinary artist from Austria. Her work mediates between art and science, fashion and science, design and science, between clothes and body, between fiction and facts. Although she has a background in fashion design and design, her projects are not bound by a defined field. She allows herself to freely explore the subjects she treats, thereby allowing unexpected results to occur. In 2012 Bäumel was awarded an *Outstanding Artist Award Experimental Design* from the Federal Ministry for Education, Art and Culture in Vienna. She lives and works in Amsterdam and Vienna. For more, visit: www.sonjabaeumel.at.

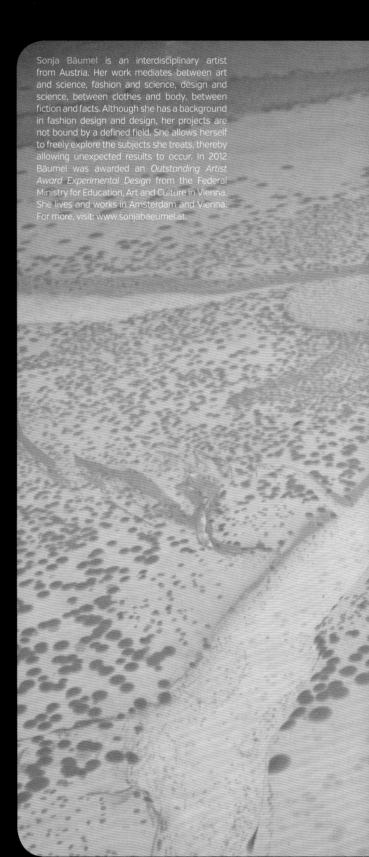

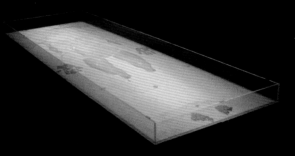

SONJA BÄUMEL
FEATURE ARTIST

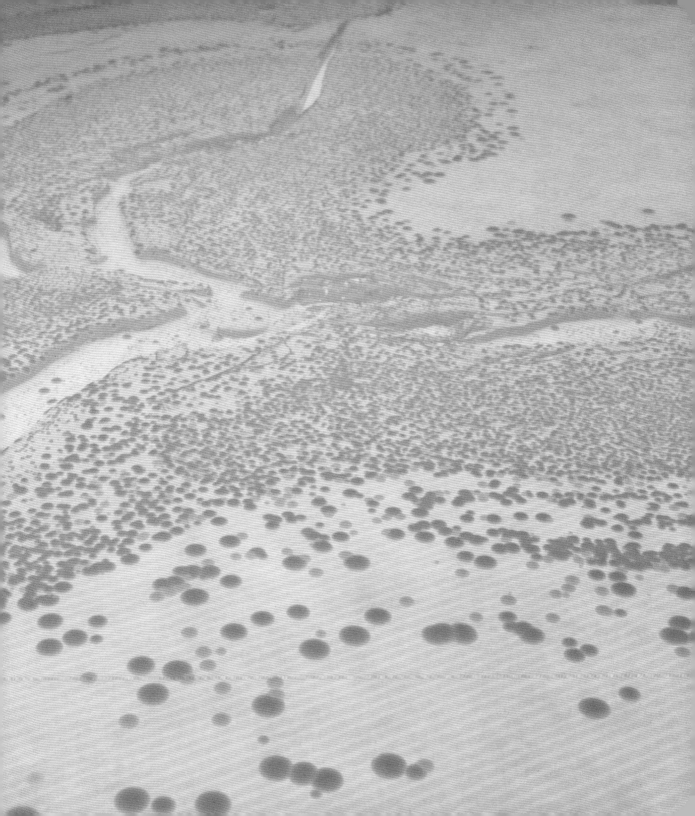

ROD BARNETT
UNPREMEDITATED ART

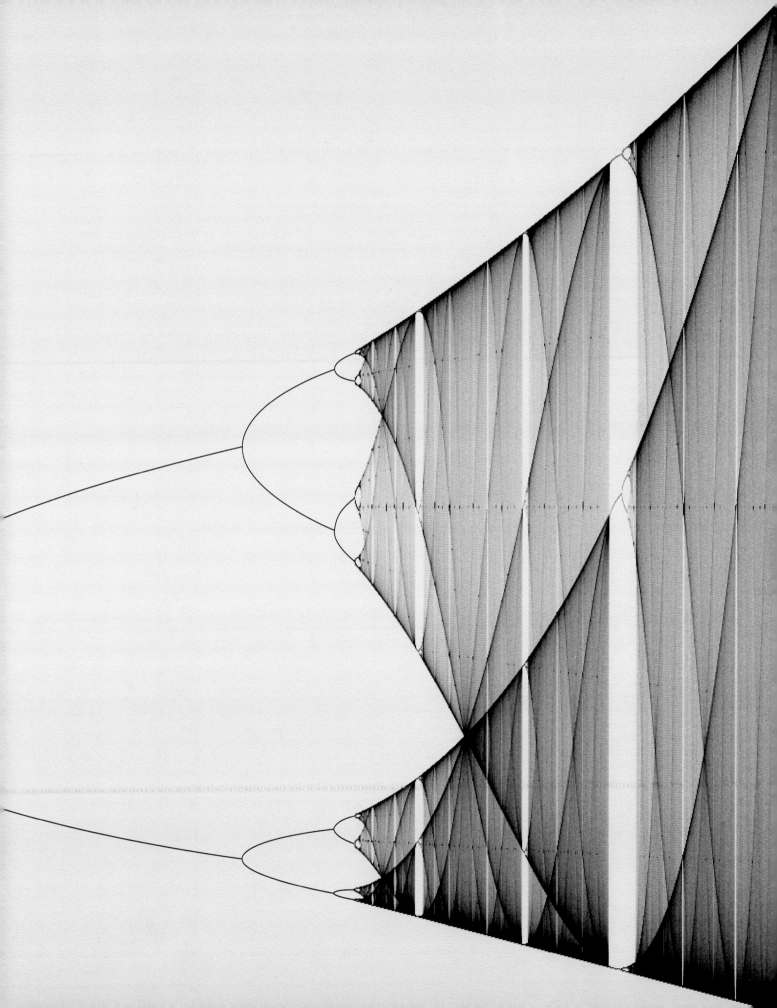

Rod Barnett is Chair of the Master of Landscape Architecture program in the Sam Fox School of Design and Visual Arts at Washington University in St Louis, Missouri. He teaches, practices, writes and draws at the intersection of the human and nonhuman, where open systems flourish and novel encounters occur.

+ AGRICULTURE, CONSERVATION, CHAOS THEORY

The skylark [Alauda arvensis], indigenous to Europe and Asia, has been introduced to North America, where it has not done well, and to other areas colonized by Europeans, such as Australia and New Zealand, where it has thrived. The European habitat was typically a biologically diverse grassland where the skylark–principally a ground-dwelling bird–could hide its nest and forage for seeds and insects. It has always been a welcome member of the republic of beings because it lends itself to easy field observation, and particularly because of the mating behavior of the male.[1] This involves a rapid ascent to a great height such that the bird is a speck in the sky, and then a slow spiraling descent accompanied by a thrilling, cascading song that fills the air with hope and joy.

The Eurasian Skylark population went into steep decline with the advent of industrial agriculture and the changing production regimes that accompanied large-scale, market-driven cropping. Its plight demonstrates once again the vulnerability of open systems to catastrophic change. In *The End of Certainty*, the Nobel Prize-winning chemist Ilya Prigogine describes emergent systems as at their most vital when they are pushed to *far-from-equilibrium* conditions by their interaction with other dynamic forces. All open systems, from ecosystems to cities are emergent systems. "[T]he universe itself is highly heterogeneous and far-from-equilibrium. This prevents systems from reaching a state of equilibrium. For example, the flow of energy that originates in the irreversible nuclear reactions within the sun maintains our systems far from equilibrium and has thus made it possible for life to develop on earth."[2] Disequilibrium implies irreversibility, instability, uncertainty, and extreme openness to perturbation. In 1881 the British poet George Meredith wrote "The Lark Ascending," in which this condition is described as follows:

> He rises and begins to round,
> He drops the silver chain of sound
> Of many links without a break,
> In chirrup, whistle, slur and shake,
> All intervolv'd and spreading wide,
> Like water-dimples down a tide
> Where ripple ripple overcurls
> And eddy into eddy whirls;
> A press of hurried notes that run
> So fleet they scarce are more than one.

The male lark, high in the air, 50 to 100 meters from the ground, sings for up to 20 minutes in the mating season, hovering on wings that have broadened through adaptation to female skylarks' preference for males that can sing in suspended animation for long periods of time. The 16 centimeter skylark occupies a far-from-equilibrium condition. It commits itself to a steady, "intervol'd" downward drift as energy courses through the many internal and external systems that push the small bird through moments of instability and transformation. Meredith's poem highlights the lark's capacity, as this occurs, to spontaneously emit melodic song structures of extraordinary complexity and continuous novelty.

Larks, like all biological species, are disequilibrious open systems. As science writer Mitchell Waldrop points out, "it is extremely meaningless to talk about a complex adaptive system being in equilibrium: the system can never get there. It is always unfolding, always in transition. In fact if the system does reach equilibrium it isn't just stable. It's dead."[3] Open systems are necessarily unstable. The more open a nonhuman system is, the further it is from human ambition, from prediction, from value, from reason, from the reductivism of science and society. Open systems don't care. Their ontology has nothing to do with human beings.

To be far from equilibrium, then, is to be wild. To be wild is to exist in a condition of extreme openness – instability, uncertainty, and continual perturbation. And yet to be wild is not something that humans can achieve: it is unknowable. In other words, if something is knowable, it is not wild.

How do we enwild our world when we cannot know the wild? Surely we cannot draw the nonhuman into our world unless we make that world open to the wild? It is only when we find out what larks actually connect to that we can make a world for larks. We have to understand what captivates them. One of the founders of ecology, the biologist Jacob Von Uexküll, argued that the environment–or *Umvelt*–of any animal is defined by what he called "carriers of significance."[4] These are the specific things to which it connects through its need for food, shelter, and procreation. The *Umvelt* of a lark stretches from the open sky to tufts of grass in a broad field. While this seamless milieu may not appear to be a particularly exacting requirement, nevertheless the carriers of significance that comprise it form an exclusive, reciprocal, and inextricably linked chain of elements that really is the only thing that interests the lark. Uexküll saw these components as "melodies in counterpoint," and nature itself as "a gigantic musical score."[5] The lark's song, in Meredith's phrase "an ecstasy to music turned," is a perfect contribution to the score.[6]

The Royal Society for the Protection of Birds (RSPB) has been measuring this contribution by means of a bird census started in the early 1960s. The census shows that current lark numbers in the United Kingdom are only 10% of what they were 30 years ago. In the past, cereals were planted in the spring, grown in the summer, and harvested in the early fall. For reasons to do with global market forces, cereals are now planted in the fall, grown through the winter, and harvested in the early summer. The winter-grown fields are much too dense in summer for walking skylarks to forage between the stems for seeds and insects. Additionally, studies of skylark populations in England and Germany show that territory density varies considerably according to crop type, compactness, and height.[7] Also important is the intensity and timing of pesticide use, and whether the pasture is grazed between cropping. Single-species cropping reduces the structural diversity of agrarian terrains, pesticides kill insects, and intensive management interferes with the territorial requirements of the birds.[8]

Field ecology research has suggested that setting aside sufficiently large and numerous areas of otherwise commercially farmed fields, and reducing regrowth within these zones, can help to increase suitable nesting opportunities for skylarks and thereby improve breeding success.[9] As a result, farmers in England are now paid to maintain and create biodiversity for increasing the habitat of skylarks. Studies, conducted initially by RSPB, and more extensively by the Sustainable Arable Farming for an Improved Environment Project (SAFFIE), have shown that suitable nesting sites for larks can be made during the sowing of commercial crops, by turning the seeding machine off (or lifting the drill) for a five- to ten-meter stretch as the tractor goes over the ground, to briefly stop the seeds from being sown. Repeated in several areas in the same field to make about two skylark plots per acre, these "seed tables" enable breeding skylarks access to multiple foraging opportunities, even within a wider regime of poor crop mosaics and continued spraying and fertilizing operations.[10]

The results from this large consortium-led research program (funded amongst others by the Agricultural Industries Confederation and Sainsbury's Supermarkets Ltd) have suggestive implications for the ongoing reformation of rural areas. They bring the high-tech economic imperatives of the contemporary world into an expansive social and spatial continuum in which ordinary humans and delicate wild species may overlap and fuse. Skylark plots open up not only a network of physical spaces that can be appreciated by humans for their aesthetic and affective qualities, but an uncertain and fragile "golden cup" of indigenous (and sometimes introduced) species of plants, insects, and small mammals. When the wheat crop grows, the skylark plots become zones of low vegetation where larks can easily hunt insects and build their well-camouflaged ground nests. These areas are also good for other ground-dwelling avian species such as pheasants and partridge, species that, with skylarks, emblematize the organic regionalism grounded in land use, husbandry, and rural mythologies that encouraged 20th-century ruralists to consider the whole of a region as a work of art.[11]

The skylark initiative has the potential to operate across extensive territories of English (and European) farmland, linking small, individual, unseeded (even untilled) zones of skylark habitat within an open system of patches and corridors, that have been spared Jethro Tull's benedictions (for it was he who invented the seed drill).

A combination of top-down and bottom-up activism, it's an integrated effort at skylark recovery that involves multinational companies such as KGT and Agriterra,[12] their financial strategists, PR departments, farm managers, and—importantly—their tractor operators, as well as rural communities, and even urban hikers, in the linked but essentially uncoordinated production of designed landscape conditions.

If implemented on the scale of districts and regions, the project could have fascinating outcomes. But the future spatial, ecological, and even social patterns of rural English farmland that may result from such a simple initial action as lifting seed drills for a few seconds are not actually able to be determined. Embedded, or nested, within countywide webs of agrarian structure and process, the skylark project offers a matrix of habitats that together form a shifting, drifting network of feeding and breeding opportunities which are otherwise being lost. Over several years the locations and sizes of the skylark plots would necessarily change, as the project evolves and practices develop in different directions. The ecology of *Alauda arvensis*, however, has its own speeds and rhythms: precise timings of mating, nesting, breeding, and raising fledglings. It would be critical that these rhythms are combined within the corporative imperatives of crop production, management, and harvesting.

1 "Republic of beings" is Bruno Latour's phrase. Latour has argued for an assembly of human and nonhuman "actants" within a broad social democracy that does not value species on the basis of their difference from humans (see his *The Politics of Nature: How to Bring the Sciences into Democracy* (Cambridge, Mass: Harvard University Press, 2004).

2 Ilya Prigogine, *The End of Certainty: Time, Chaos and the New Laws of Nature* (New York: The Free Press, 1996), 158.

3 M. Mitchell Waldrop, *Complexity: The Emerging Science at the Edge of Order and Chaos* (New York: Simon and Schuster Paperbacks, 1992), 147.

4 Giorgio Agamben, *The Open: Man and Animal* (2004) 40.

5 Gilles Deleuze & Felix Guattari, *A Thousand Plateaus: Capitalism and Schizophrenia* (Minnesota: University of Minnesota Press, 1987) 315; Agamben (2004) 40.

6 George Meredith, "The Lark Ascending" (1881).

7 Jeremy D. Wilson, Julianne Evans, Stephen J. Browne, and Jon R. King, "Territory Distribution and Breeding Success of Skylarks Alauda Arvensis on Organic and Intensive Farmland in Southern England," *Journal of Applied Ecology* 34 (1997): 1462–78, 1476.

8 Ibid.

9 Ibid; see also J.G. Poulson, "Behavioural and Parental Care of Skylark Alauda Arvensis Chicks" *Ibis* 138 (1996): 525–31.

10 "Skylark Plots," The Royal Society for the Protection of Birds, 2004, www.rspb.org.uk (accessed 29 June 2014). See also Morris et al., "Sustainable Arable Farming for an Improved Environment Project: Managing winter wheat sward structure for skylarks" *Ibis* 146 (Suppl. 2) (2004): 155–162.

11 See David Matless, *Landscape and Englishness* (London, Reaktion Books, 1998) for an extended, insightful discussion of the development of material landscape cultures in England.

12 Khalsan General Trading (KGT), headquartered in Dubai, is an international foodstuffs, electronics, and petrochemical company. It trades commodities such as rice, chick peas, seeds, dried fruits, and edible oils, as well as microchips, diodes, capacitors, and bitumen, gas oil, and urea: www.khalsan. com. The Agriterra Group (assets $57.5m) is a consortium of pan-African agricultural companies processing beef, cocoa, maize, palm oil, and other farmed and cropped products. Its business strategy is to become one of the largest agri-operators in Africa: www.agriterra-ltd.com.

13 Nick Groom, *The Seasons: An Elegy for the Passing Year* (London: Atlantic Books, 2013).

14 Percy Bysshe Shelley, "To a Skylark," in A.S.B. Glover (ed.), *Shelley: Selected Prose, Poetry and Letters* (London: The Nonesuch Press, 1951).

Most countries have a considerable, and loved, catalogue of rural histories and place-based rural micro-cultures. These are still in some shape or form *lived* although, as Nick Groom advises in *The Seasons*, they need to be lived afresh through today's experiences and values.[13] The collective of human and nonhuman beings continues to come together in country places without the husbandry of landscape architectural design, and are gathered by tradition, weather, and patterns of interaction between beasts, birds, and–these days–stockbrokers. It is easy to take an oppositional approach to changes in our shared rural patrimony, particularly the advent of agribusiness. The skylark project is an attempt to foreground inherited patterns, but within a network of cohabitation and encounter that firmly claims rural public space as a constructed realm. It suggests that large-scale agrarian infrastructure offers opportunities for the continuing development of the working countryside as an assemblage of production, observation, interaction, and enhancement that can achieve a multitude of goals.

In his 1820 poem "To a Skylark," Shelley refers to the song of this much-loved bird as an "unpremeditated art."[14] The phrase describes an open system that creates novelty through its encounter with indeterminate conditions. It is a useful way to consider the potential of the SAFFIE project as it drifts across the English countryside like the lark's "silver chain" of notes "all intervolv'd and spreading wide." Even though it is regulated by the structural parameters of the bird's body and its organs, for walkers in the fields of Britain and Europe the song of the skylark is the spontaneous production of an open condition, far from equilibrium, a condition we call wild, that does not exist for us. It is the production of a small, brown bird of which Shelley declares, "What thou art we know not."

Abalone (per kilogram) African Grey Parrot Arowana Fish Australian Lizard Baby Elephant – in Thailand

Clouded Leopard – in China Elephant Elephant Tusk – in Vietnam Frog Legs (12 pairs) – in France Gecko [f

Ivory (with carvings) Komodo Dragon Leopard Leopard Tortoise Monkey – in Europe Monkey – in

Panther Ploughshare Tortoise Polar Bear (skin) Rhino Horn Dagger Rhino Horn (per kilogram)

Spotted Salamander Tiger Tiger Bone Tiger Bone Wine Tiger Penis Tiger Remains – in China Tiger S

TRADING WILD: This page documents the prices (in US Dollars) of wildlife on the black market today. Source: www.havocscope.

Bear Bile (per pound)   Bear Paws (set of 4)   Black Cockatoo   Butterfly (Queen Alexandra)   Chimpanzee

aland) – in Europe   Gecko – in the Philippines   Gila Monster   Gorilla   Iguana   Ivory – in Asia

Orangutan   Owl – in India   Pangolin   Pangolin Meat (per kilogram)   Pangolin Scales (per kilogram)

Sloth – in Columbia   Snake Venom (per liter)   Snake (Banded Krait)   Snow Leopard Pelt – in Afghanistan

ortoises – in Madagascar   Totoaba Fish Bladder – in China   Turtle (Chinese Golden Coin)   Turtle Eggs – in Costa Rica

JULIAN RAXWORTHY
BORN TO BE WILD:
HEAT LEAKS, AND THE WRONG SORT OF REWILDING

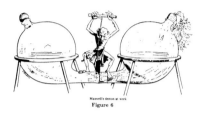

Maxwell's demon at work
Figure 6

Julian Raxworthy is a Lecturer in the Master of Landscape Architecture program at the University of Cape Town. He completed his PhD with the University of Queensland, Australia in 2013, concerning the relationship between gardening and landscape architecture, in regard to change. He co-edited *The MESH Book: Landscape & Infrastructure*, and co-authored *Sunburnt: Landscape Architecture in Australia*.

✛ THERMODYNAMICS, ECOLOGY, DESIGN

Rewilding, which George Monbiot describes as "the re-introduction of animal and plant species to habitats from which they had been excised," would seem at first glance to be a very Anthropocene concept which, like geoengineering, accepts that since we have already modified the environment ecologically we can, or rather must, continue to intervene deliberately.[1] But either way, to intervene or not intervene still rests upon an ideological sub-division of nature and culture. Instead of imposing an ideological overlay on ecological process, in this essay I propose using energy—described in thermodynamic terms—as a language that unites (and indeed does not distinguish between) people and the environment. Seen in terms of energy, I use the practices of Dutch artist Louis Le Roy and English scientist-gardener Geoffrey Dutton in their 'gardens', as examples of how gardening can be a model for working productively with existing ecological processes.

I refer to the preference for a particular date-stamped state of the environment (for rewilding, the pre-human) as ideological because it assumes that there is a right and a wrong state, whereas ecology teaches us that everything is ecological, regardless of what humans might think about it. From my own experience of the Gondwanan colonies (Australia, South America and, more recently, South Africa), this ideology can be commonly seen where ecological restoration welcomes regeneration—when its ideological frame is redemption—since it is concerned with restoring an indigenous order, but is undesirable when such spontaneous vegetation is non-indigenous "weeds," which are nonetheless an ecological response. From my Gondwanan perspective, Monbiot's view of wilderness is nostalgic because it fails to recognize that even seemingly pristine pre-white settlement wildernesses were in fact manipulated in a way that resembles gardening. In the Amazon, for example, plants were introduced into created forest clearings and then abandoned,[2] while in Australia, Aboriginal people used fire to manipulate grasslands to encourage macropod grazing.[3] Both these practices work economically with existing landscape processes to spontaneously create the same ecological outcomes as rewilding. In them, plants occupy niches on the basis of entirely non-ideological thermodynamic transfer processes that are already operational in ecological systems responding to disturbance in an ongoing fashion.

Thinking thermodynamically is a useful way to think about ecology because it removes the limits around systems, including the limits that are overlaid by particular ecological ideologies about what the appropriate ecological state is. When Monbiot says that "the ecosystems that result are best described not as wilderness, but as self-willed: governed not by human management but by their own processes,"[4] this suggests that human intervention is somehow assisting the teleological desires of nature. Thermodynamics instead focuses on flow throughout the broader energy system across ecological states and welcomes the unintended consequences from state change as a description of the ecological system, rather than of a particular "order" or "material organization." Seen in the light of constant and irreversible state change, the desire for a particular ecological order is the creation of a boundary around an ecology; however, this is impossible because energy *leaks* from a given system of any type to the systems surrounding it.

Dutch artist and teacher Louis G. Le Roy noted that "for anyone who thinks and works ecologically, the most important aspect is the management of energy."[5] Between the late 1970s and his death in 2012, Le Roy constructed what he called an "Ecocathedral," near Heerenveen in the Netherlands, from recycled masonry salvaged from dumping by the local council. Artfully stacked by hand without tools or mortar, and leaving gaps for "nature," over 30 years an empty agricultural field became a biodiverse forest due to a combination of naturalization of introduced species and spontaneous vegetation that thrived in the diverse microclimates created by the brick stacks.

Le Roy was inspired by a book by Nobel Prize–winner Ilya Prigogine and Isabelle Stengers entitled *Order out of Chaos*, which concerns the thermodynamics of nonequilibrium systems, of which life is an example.[6] Since energy is never destroyed, "thermodynamics" essentially refers to how energy is transferred. This is called the First Law of Thermodynamics, which accompanies a change of state of the energy, from water to steam, for example. The Second Law of Thermodynamics describes how "entropy" increases as this change of state occurs. Entropy is often called "disorder" but it could really be described as a change in utility. This is because the application of thermodynamics originally aimed at limiting these state changes to get as much use (or work, as it is called) out of the energy as possible, classically in a steam engine. Theoretically, entropy increases until the system reaches equilibrium, when it becomes static or unchanging.[7] However, no system can truly reach equilibrium because, according to the First Law, the energy keeps transferring.[8] While this was a problem

for classical thermodynamics, for Le Roy it was a welcome, unifying factor that linked the actions of man to the environment, so that he saw his own energy expenditure in stacking resulting in growth and ecological complexity (both as biodiversity and diversity of microclimates) of the Ecocathedral.

In scientific terms, Prigogine and collaborator Dilip Kondepudi use the notion of *local equilibrium* as a way of literally measuring entropy, which relies on considering variables as functions of position and time, treating a moment as an autonomous system before it again changes state, when it becomes another system with different properties.[9] Thought of in this way, as Erwin Schrödinger writes, "entropy is itself a measure of order."[10] At the Ecocathedral, Le Roy then is *forming entropy*, a role that Luis Fernández-Galiano ascribes to architecture, which "can be understood as a *material* organization that regulates and brings order to energy *flows*."[11] However, Kondepudi and Prigogine's use of local equilibrium is really a conceptual convenience, like focusing on a lifeboat at sea, because energy is continually leaking from one system to another. Thus, while an organism seems bounded, autonomous, it "maintains itself stationary at a fairly high level of orderliness [that] really consists in continually sucking orderliness from its environment."[12] Correspondingly, the order in a system is a leak from another system, across a state change boundary. Thus, the best that can be described in an ordered way is not the thing itself, but its form in a moment of change, as its energy moves through time and space, something which Sanford Kwinter discussed in relation to Boccioni and the Futurists.[13] This notion of leakiness demonstrates that the maintenance of an ideological boundary condition around an ecological system is an attempt to constrain it in the face of its flux, which is the very thing the discourse of ecology arose to describe in the first place.

By focusing on the biodiversity of a particular historic moment, like the Pleistocene, rather than accepting that ecological systems are already operating in a normal manner, rewilding is making choices that represent a kind of cultivation, ostensibly gardening – a term that I, unlike many landscape architects, do not use pejoratively.[14] Monbiot, however, sets up rewilding specifically in opposition to conservation practices that he regards as gardening: practices that treat nature as a museum and expend energy trying to keep it in a particular state. Le Roy's use of plants (introduced and spontaneous) in the Ecocathedral is ruthless and pragmatic but, as the following suggests, arguably more "ecological:"

> Which plants are included in the system is in essence unimportant. It may be the original ones...if they can stick it out; if they can't, we'll introduce other ones indiscriminately as long as they can cope with their surrounds. In other words, I don't feel any need to create some plant-sociologically correct grouping artificially: what I want is artificial ecosystems.[15]

If one subscribes to the view that we currently occupy the Anthropocene epoch, then all ecosystems are artificial because the climate system that all ecosystems occupy is modified. Le Roy asserts that "because ecology claims to study the relational patterns of living creatures...and the environment, it is unthinkable that human beings should be excluded as creators! But increasingly human beings are being treated as spectators, while this passivity is in total contradiction with everything that is ecological."[16]

Le Roy's ecological pragmatism may allow a level of adaptation within the changing biosphere that could create novel[17] and, above all, useful ecologies by optimizing ecological niches through a gardening-like relationship to natural systems. Despite contrary suggestions, gardening is inherently ecological and its success relies on the practical catalyzation of ecological systems through gardening technique.[18] To embrace Le Roy's model is to embrace a thermodynamic pragmatism that is concerned with monitoring local conditions and intervening to increase complexity or achieve other effects.

Biomedical scientist and gardener Geoffrey Dutton would define this type of gardening practice as "marginal gardening." Like Le Roy, Dutton also saw an edgeless thermodynamic continuum between the energy of the sun, man, and the landscape:

> it is only the simple sunlight
> on a fence post
> out of the snow.
> and I come to set it upright
> at the cost
> of a single blow.
> then I leave them to the sunlight.
> one straight post,
> trodden snow.[19]

In the *Marginal Garden*, Dutton writes both about a type of garden that is marginal in terms of its location and ecology, and a type of gardening practice that could be described as marginal.[20] Dutton's garden (which was unnamed because he kept its location secret, but has been called "Duttonia" by another visitor)[21] is located in the Scottish highlands and was developed between the 1970s and Dutton's death in 2010. As a place, his garden was marginal because it was literally "at the edge of cultivation," occupying the climatic and ecological margin between a garden environment and the Arctic mountains. And further, because the existing site was already interesting, Dutton suggested it called for "marginal gardening," which "minimally differentiated [it] from its environment,"[22] requiring careful judgement about the degree of intervention:

> [I]n the jargon of ecology it was moribund and called for a healing hand. Still, restoration would invite, as always, 'meddling' (to employ a Jekyllian rebuke) and seeing what other kinds of plants would do: the deadliest temptation in a spot like this.[23]

1 George Monbiot, *Feral: Searching for Enchantment on the Frontiers of Rewilding* (London: Penguin Books, 2013), 14.

2 Philippe Descola, *In the Society of Nature: A Native Ecology in Amazonia* (Cambridge: Cambridge University Press, 1996).

3 Bill Gammage, *The Biggest Estate on Earth: How Aborigines Made Australia* (Sydney: Allen & Unwin, 2012).

4 Monbiot, *Feral: Searching for Enchantment on the Frontiers of Rewilding*, 15.

5 Louis G. Le Roy, "Coconut Palms," in E. Boukema & P.V. McIntyre (eds), *Louis G. Le Roy: Nature Culture Fusion* (Rotterdam: NAi Uitgevers, 2002), 36.

6 Ilya Priqogine & Isabelle Stengers, *Order out of Chaos* (London: Fontana, 1984).

7 Artist Robert Smithson famously described the resulting equilibrium state as a kind of "radical banality"—"a kind of architecture without values or qualities...if anything...a fact:" Robert Smithson, "Entropy and the New Monuments," in Nancy Holt (ed.), *The Writings of Robert Smithson* (New York: New York University Press, 1979), 9.

8 "Second Law thinking" has developed as a part of sustainability discourse to look at minimizing such transfers: S. Stremke, A. Van Den Dobbelsteen, & J. Koh, "Exergy Landscapes: Exploration of Second-Law Thinking Towards Sustainable Landscape Design," *International Journal of Exergy* 8, no. 2 (2011).

9 Dilip Kondepudi and Ilya Prigogine, *Modern Thermodynamics: From Heat Engines to Dissipative Structures* (Chichester: John Wiley & Sons, 1998), 87.

10 Erwin Schrödinger, *What Is Life?: The Physical Aspect of the Living Cell with Mind and Matter and Autobiographical Sketches* (Cambridge: Cambridge, 1992), 73.

11 Luis Fernández-Galiano, *Fire and Memory: On Architecture and Energy*, trans. Gina Cariño, *Writing Architecture* (Cambridge, Massachusetts: The MIT Press, 2000), 5. And "simultaneously and inseparably, as an energetic organization that stabilizes and maintains material forms."

12 Schrödinger, *What Is Life?*, 73.

13 Sanford Kwinter, "Landscapes of Change: Boccioni's Strati D'animo as a General Theory of Models," *Assemblage* 19 (1992).

14 I discuss the vital role that gardening can play to achieve unique spatial effects beyond a landscape design in Julian Raxworthy, "Gardening Forms: Landscape Architecture and Gardening in Sven-Ingvar Andersson's Garden at Marnas," *Journal of Landscape Architecture* 12 (2011).

15 Le Roy, "Coconut Palms," 36.

16 Louis G. Le Roy, "New Value," in E. Boukema & P.V. McIntyre (eds), *Louis G. Le Roy: Nature Culture Fusion* (Rotterdam: NAi Uitgevers, 2002), 68.

17 Emma Marris, *Rambunctious Garden: Saving Nature in a Post-Wild World* (New York: Bloomsbury, 2011).

Louis Le Roy's "EcoCathedral."

Geoffrey Dutton's "Duttonia."

Dutton's definition of marginal gardening is useful both because he, like Le Roy, used energy as model and criteria for considering action in relation to its result, and also because it gives a name to the kind of practice that rewilding is, recognizing that it is a gardening-like intervention that works with systems. Dutton's model of marginal gardening is focused on accepting the site as already operational or active thermodynamically and any change should be "minimally costed in gardener's energy."[24] Such meddling needs to be economical because, as he explains, "the natural forces operating here are so violent, the vegetation exploiting them so precisely selected, and the biological equilibrium therefore so finely poised, that a gardener is rapidly taught humility."[25] This sense of biological equilibrium recalls Prigogine's consideration of the organism amongst the laws of thermodynamics, when Dutton describes the cell as a membrane moderating the environment: "this island in the flux was thereby enabled to create its own flux, interdependent with the external one; it became a living system extracting energy from its environment for its own maintenance and growth."

Once one takes on a thermodynamic approach to energy, the questions that I am arguing plague rewilding–primarily concerning the contradiction between ideological preference for "original" conditions and a dispassionate, practical assessment of ecological change–disappear. Like Kondepudi and Prigogine's definition of local equilibrium, Dutton takes a calm and pragmatic view of the form of the garden as a provisional state of energy at a particular point in time, and thus "a marginal garden can be made anywhere and to any degree of formality, consistent with minimal input of energy."[26] Recognizing a plant is an organism that exercises a level of judgement about its locations in terms of how it responds to it (what Michael Marder would call "plant thinking"),[27] Dutton sees native plants that might seem to be the secret of the marginal garden as "satisfying but infuriating creatures. The infuriating part is when you find out–while your back has been turned–the 'natives' have gone: either vanished into carbon dioxide, or busy invading their neighbour's territory, with havoc on both sides."[28] Rather than downplaying intervention in the marginal garden, like Le Roy, intervention, however slight, is the key because it activates the site: "[the marginal garden] is not differentiated from the wild [until it has] some other manifestation of the gardener's intent."[29] The specificity of the interaction between the act and the reaction of the environment is a feature of marginal gardening, as it is of rewilding; and while the latter rejects gardening, I would argue that, in Dutton's terms, it is an appropriate description of how rewilding can operate.

In this essay I have sought to embrace the willfulness and magnitude of the concept of rewilding but to reject its nostalgia for a pre-human ecological condition. This is necessary because while ecology will be the tool for rewilding, in itself ecology has no preference for a particular state apart from that which works. To avoid such ideological overlays on ecology while embracing the ambition and magnitude of rewilding, I have instead adopted thermodynamics as a more neutral way of describing ecological systems that highlights their flux. By using the work of Le Roy and Dutton as case studies I have sought to demonstrate that acting economically and optimizing the effects of thermodynamic transfer is a model that could be used for rewilding. Taking a designerly, but nonetheless ethical, view of these kinds of interventions allows for a liberation of energy and the development of exciting and novel ecologies that move landscape design to act on systems in a way that resembles the notion of gardening it rejects.

18 Stefan Buczaki, *Ground Rules for Gardeners: A Practical Guide to Garden Ecology* (London: Collins, 1986).

19 Anne Stevenson, "Geoffrey Dutton Obituary," *The Guardian*, http://www.theguardian.com/science/2010/jul/20/geoffrey-dutton-obituary (accessed 20 June 2014).

20 Geoffrey Dutton, *Some Branch against the Sky: The Practice and Principles of Marginal Gardening* (Devon: David & Charles, 1997).

21 Alec Finlay, "Duttonia: Framed Wilderness," Skying, http://skying-blog.blogspot.com/2011/12/duttonia-framed-wilderness.html (accessed 20 June 2014).

22 Dutton, *Some Branch against the Sky*, 166.

23 Ibid., 14.

24 Ibid., 166.

25 Ibid., 14.

26 Ibid., 167.

27 Michael Marder, *Plant-Thinking: A Philosophy of Vegetal Life* (New York: Columbia University Press, 2013).

28 Dutton, *Some Branch against the Sky*, 122.

29 Ibid., 165.

NATURE IS NEVER FINISHED.

- Robert Smithson

STEVE PYNE

FIRESCAPING

Steve Pyne is a Senior Sustainability Scientist, Environmental historian at Arizona State University and leading author on the history, ecology, and management of fire.

✚ FIRE MANAGEMENT, ECOLOGY, ENVIRONMENTAL HISTORY

F ire is peculiar, and to consider it as a landscaping feature may seem beyond quirky. After all, among the ancient elements it is the odd one out. Earth is a solid and can be sculpted directly. Water and air are fluids, but still substances, and their flow can be stored, channeled, or otherwise manipulated. All can be moved with their essence intact from one site to another. But fire is a reaction, not a substance. Its setting makes it possible. It synthesizes its surroundings. It takes its character from its context. Fire is landscape, and airshed, and watershed, integrated.

We think we control fire by starting it and, within limits, stopping it. After all, we can't spark earth or water or air into existence—we can fire. Not only do we control ignition, we are the only creature that does. We hold a species monopoly over one of Earth's most elemental phenomena. Our firepower is who we are.

The power of fire, however, resides in its power to propagate. We don't really hold or carry fire, we carry the ingredients that sustain it; so fire doesn't spread as a wolf might lope over hills or water rush down a ravine. Fire can only propagate if its setting allows: it literally feeds off its context. We think we control fire by quenching it; and in select circumstances, where fire is small and contained, this is possible. We cool the reaction zone, smother airflow, remove fuels, or interrupt the heat flux that must continue unbroken if fire is to persist. Without the capacity to spread, the fire extinguishes.

But move to larger landscapes and none of this is possible. You must cool with planeloads of water or retardant. You must cut fuelbreaks the size of roads or football fields (the rule of thumb is that the fuel-free zone should be 1.5 times as wide as the flames are high) and that doesn't account for embers blown by high winds across firelines with no more pause than water over Niagara Falls. That's what makes wildland fire control so difficult, expensive, and damaging. The firescape must be altered dramatically under emergency conditions.

Today, the United States and cognate fire countries have extensive wildland fires because they have extensive wildlands. Most of these wildlands are the outcome of political decisions under a philosophy of state-sponsored conservation. But you can create similar conditions by letting land go to seed. Abandoned, former agricultural lands are powering the flareup of wildfires—or more properly, feral fires—around the Mediterranean Basin and increasingly in parts of the developed world generally.

There is a double paradox here. The first is that most of these lands were set aside to spare them, in the language of the day, "from fire and ax;" instead they became permanent habitats for fire. The second is that they often need fire: just not in the unprecedented form too many of them are getting. The evolving fire regimes of the 21st century may threaten ecological goods and services as much as landclearing by fire and ax did in the 19th

The fire scene is likely to worsen. The legacy of fuels from the past that feed megafires, the global economy of present times that is for the developed world recolonizing rural lands with suburbs, and the changing climate forecast for the future will in many places combine to yield unstoppable fires. A fire scene thought banished into the past may reappear like a reemergent plague.

Still, much remains under our control. We can tweak those legacy fuels. We don't have to revert to commodity production or the excesses of clearcutting and overgrazing that Teddy Roosevelt once described as "scalping" the land. Logging, for example, takes the big stuff and leaves the little; fire burns the little and leaves the big. Logging physically removes biomass; fire chemically transmutes it. They are inverse, not surrogate, processes. Instead, we should think about new varieties of working landscapes sculpted for ecological goods and services. With those fuels rearranged, you can substitute tame fire for wild or can repurpose free-burning flame. While control is never complete—the task can resemble teaching a grizzly bear to dance—humanity has long practiced it.

We can protect our built landscape where it abuts the wild. We know how to keep houses from burning. Moreover, research repeatedly demonstrates that most structures burn from ember attacks, not tsunamis of flame. Relatively simple design features and near-structure landscaping can reduce losses. Modest landscaping into the pyric equivalent of greenbelts can push the threat further away. After all, our cities used to burn as often as their surroundings; now they don't. The same methods, adapted, can work along the fractal frontier of exurban settlement.

And while we can't counter climate change so easily, it's important to note that flaming forests are not simply the flip-side of melting glaciers. Ice melts from purely physical causes, while climate must refract through complex biotas and societies. All those contributing factors provide points of intervention that are not possible in icefields. It's worth recalling, too, that anthropogenic climate change—the Anthropocene, for that matter—is a product of humanity's change in combustion habits.

We began burning the fuels of fossilized landscapes instead of living ones. We yet remain Earth's keystone species for fire.

The instinctive response to a fire threat is to muster larger counter-forces. More crews. More engines. More airtankers and helicopters. This, however, only responds to the immediate crisis, not to the circumstances that make such fires possible. A century ago we attempted to exclude fire in our reserved wildlands. In places outside temperate Europe where fire is a natural phenomenon, and even in central Europe where cultural landscapes like heaths have become valued, that strategy was a mistake. The true issue is not whether fire will exist, but what kind of fire. A firefight can only suppress a temporary environmental insurrection: it cannot govern. We control fire's regime by controlling its setting. We substitute fires we can live with for those we can't.

That we have not responded to fire's challenge on anything like the scale required speaks to considerations of economics, aesthetics, exurban sprawl and, of course, politics. As fire synthesizes everything in its surroundings, so economics and politics synthesize those considerations that guide human decisions about land use. It probably is no accident that in developed countries landscapes have polarized into the wild and the urban at the expense of a working middle, or that fire policies have likewise split into incommensurate moieties, at the same time, for example, as the American economy and the American polity have. We can't devise appropriate landscapes because we can't agree on what we want those public lands to be or, in the case of private lands, what kind of regulations we are willing to impose. Fire doesn't care. It will synthesize whatever is there.

Yet precisely because it integrates everything, the scene abounds in levers and handholds. How to fashion such settings without exorbitant costs or nuked landscapes or political gridlock is a challenge. But it seems one that landscape architects are particularly well placed to address.

STEFAN RAHMSTORF
WILD OCEAN

Stefan Rahmstorf is a physicist and climatologist. He is currently head of Earth System Analysis at the Potsdam Institute for Climate Impact Research in Germany and Professor of Physics of the Oceans at Potsdam University. From 2004–2013 he served on the German Advisory Council on Global Change (WBGU). Rahmstorf is an Honorary Fellow of the University of Wales and Fellow of the American Geophysical Union. He has authored over 90 scientific papers and several books, including *Our Threatened Oceans* and *The Climate Crisis*.

✛ CLIMATE SCIENCE, OCEANOGRAPHY, MARINE BIOLOGY

The global ocean is far from a pristine wilderness. Human activities have transformed the oceans in profound and lasting ways. In fact, in the past 50 years we have triggered changes in the oceans that are bigger than anything experienced for millions of years.[1] In a recent book, Katherine Richardson and I described two futures for the global ocean: a bleak one and an optimistic one.[2] Our dark vision was of an ocean in further decline, heated up by global warming, acidified by carbon dioxide, with dying coral reefs, more oil spills like that of Deepwater Horizon, widespread ecosystem collapse, algal blooms and jellyfish instead of fish. Eating wild fish would become an expensive luxury commodity for the lucky few, and rising seas would erode away beaches, overtop coastal defences during storms and force us to abandon cities and once populated islands. It is easy to arrive at such a bleak vision by just looking at what is already happening. After several millennia of stability, sea levels started rising in the late 19th century and are now rising at a rate of three centimetres each decade – three times as fast as in the early 20th century. It takes rather more imagination to see the brighter path that is open to us.

The human transformation of the oceans has been going on for so long that people living today cannot remember what was lost, how plentiful our seas once were. This is known as the shifting baselines syndrome. Ocean historians, who trawl ancient records and log books, tell us astonishing and moving tales of bays that were so full of fish one could have almost walked across them, or oyster reefs so plentiful that they formed a shipping hazard.[3] In the meantime, we have mostly emptied out the oceans and destroyed most of this abundance of life.

In one sense we still treat the ocean like the wild, though: we exploit marine life in hunter-gatherer mode. And often enough as poachers – illegal, unreported or unregulated fisheries make up between one-seventh and one-third of global catches.[4] But modern hunters use satellites and electronic fish finders to locate even the last fish in the ocean emptiness. And they use huge nets, dragged along the ocean floor, destroying everything in their way. This is rather like hunting for deer with a net by dragging down an entire forest from an air ship – this would be unthinkable on land, simply because there the collateral damage would be visible.

The health and survival of our oceans depends on us taking an active, thoughtful stewardship role rather than letting marine exploitation run wild. We need to stop treating the world ocean like a garbage dump and resource mine. We need to become more like gardeners, as we already do in many cases on land. Ultimately it is us who suffer the consequences of our reckless neglect of the health of the seas. If we keep polluting the seas, littering them with plastics and acidifying them with carbon dioxide, we should not be surprised when entire ecosystems collapse and dead zones are spreading. If we keep heating up the globe, the seas will inevitably rise further at an accelerating rate, drowning cities and entire island nations including much of our cherished heritage as humans.[5]

The oceans are a common heritage of mankind. This idea was put forward as early as the 1960s by Arvid Pardo and Elisabeth Mann Borgese in the negotiations on the United Nations Convention on the Law of the Sea. The oceans need to be governed based on this recognition, keeping them in good condition for future generations. Fully implementing this "common heritage" concept in the Law of the Sea may seem utopian today, but in fact the basis for this is already in the law – though it currently applies only to the bottom of the high seas. It needs to be extended to all but the territorial waters of coastal nations.[6] The many initiatives working on specific projects for sustainable use of the oceans could add this to their long-term agenda: building a groundswell of support for such visionary reform of the Law of the Sea.

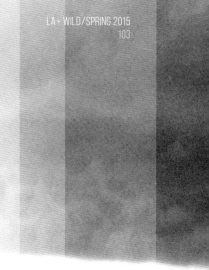

The oceans can offer many opportunities if managed properly. They can help to feed a growing population if we succeed in rebuilding depleted fish stocks and developing sustainable forms of marine aquaculture – designs of spherical cages floating freely in the ocean with the current have already been tested.[7] The oceans can help to provide us with clean, climate-friendly electricity from offshore wind (including from floating platforms), ocean currents, or waves. Of these, wind has the largest potential: even using only the technology available today, it would greatly exceed the current global demand for electricity.[8]

The oceans can also help us to store electricity – a key technology needed in a future world driven by a 100% renewable but fluctuating energy supply. This can be achieved by large hollow balls made of concrete situated on the ocean floor at great depths. Water is pumped out when excess electricity is available, and let back in through a turbine when power is needed. This works like pump storage on land – but many times more effectively due to the large water pressure available at the ocean floor. Prototypes of these devices are being built in Germany and the US.[9] Another option is wind gas – using surplus electricity at offshore wind farms for first producing hydrogen from water through electrolysis, then combining it with CO_2 from the air to make methane. While such uses of the oceans do not come free of environmental impacts (which need to be carefully evaluated), these are much smaller than those of a continuation of the fossil fuel age – both in direct impacts from offshore drilling in increasingly deep waters and the Arctic, and the indirect but pervasive double whammy of global warming and acidification.

New multi-use platforms are also being designed combining renewable-energy generation, aquaculture, transport services, and leisure activities[10] – why not use the foundations of offshore wind farms as artificial reefs and farm fish and algae amongst the windmills? With increasing pressures on the limited coastal ocean areas we need to think about such synergies and, as fishing typically does not happen in amongst offshore wind farms, these could become effective fish sanctuaries.

To get our oceans into a better state again, we need to think long term and systemically, understanding the global ocean as an ecosystem and a crucial and beautiful part of the larger Earth system. We need to act in a precautionary way, taking uncertainties that might work against us into account. We need to cooperate to overcome the tragedy of the commons, rather than following just our short-term self-interest.

The future of planet Earth's oceans is open, and it depends on us.

1 Bärbel Hönisch, et al. "The Geological Record of Ocean Acidification," Science 335, no. 6072 (2012) 335: 1058–1063.

2 Stefan Rahmstorf & Katherine Richardson, Our Threatened Oceans (London: Haus Publishing, 2009).

3 Callum W. Roberts, Ocean of Life. How Our Seas are Changing (London: Penguin, 2012).

4 David J. Agnew, et al. "Estimating the Worldwide Extent of Illegal Fishing," PLoS ONE 4, no. 2 (2009): e4570–e4577.

5 German Advisory Council on Global Change (WGBU), The Future Oceans - Warming Up, Rising High, Turning Sour (Berlin: WBGU, 2006).

6 WGBU, Governing the Marine Heritage (Berlin: WBGU, 2013).

7 Kampachi Farms, "Further and Deeper – Developing Technology for Next Generation.

8 WGBU, Governing the Marine Heritage.

9 Ibid.

10 B.H. Buck, G. Krause & H. Rosenthal, "Extensive Open Ocean Aquaculture Development within Wind Farms in Germany: the prospect of offshore co-management and legal constraints," Ocean & Coastal Management 47 no. 3–4 (2004): 95–122.

BILLY FLEMING
CAN WE REBUILD BY DESIGN?

BIG Team, "Retractable Flood Barrier."

Billy Fleming is a doctoral fellow in City and Regional Planning at the University of Pennsylvania. His research explores the relationships between design and risk management in coastal cities.

+ DESIGN, CLIMATE SCIENCE, RESILIENCE THEORY

Can we rebuild by design? This question emerged from the chaos and carnage of Superstorm Sandy during the fall of 2012. New York, the nation's most densely-populated region, appeared wholly unprepared for the relatively mild storm: subway service ceased as tunnels submerged, economic activity ground to a halt as portions of Manhattan lost power for several days, and several coastal communities faced wholesale erasure. The region's recent history, replete with near misses and false alarms,[1] helps explain why Sandy proved so destructive.[2] Though it differs considerably from the environmental history of New Orleans, the Crescent City proved equally incapable of bracing for Hurricanes Katrina and Rita in 2005.[3] After Katrina, a cadre of urban designers, policy-makers, and scholars began to explore the construct of resilience as a framework for the city's recovery. Their work called for distributed, multi-functional infrastructural systems capable of delivering flood-protection, ecological function, and social cohesion.[4] But political corruption and ineptitude left much of this work mired in the depths of theoretical abstraction and unbuilt design proposals.[5] After Sandy, the City of New York, the U.S. Department of Housing and Urban Development (HUD), and a network of non-profit institutions led by the Rockefeller Foundation began working to ensure a different story would unfold across the Northeast.[6]

First, the City of New York, led by then-Mayor Michael Bloomberg, initiated the Special Initiative for Rebuilding and Resiliency (SIRR), a planning effort resulting in 250 recommendations for protecting the city's coastlines at a cost of $19.5 billion.[7] But the city's mayoral succession cast doubt over the SIRR's future which, even if fully-implemented, would struggle to alter the regional landscape of risk. This led the Hurricane Sandy Rebuilding Task Force to reimagine the federal role in disaster recovery.[8] The Task Force's resulting recommendations culminated in the four-stage design competition known as Rebuild by Design (Rebuild). The competition received considerable praise from the press, which inspired HUD to launch the National Disaster Resilience Competition in the summer of 2014.[9]

But as HUD rushes to replicate Rebuild's model, a critical question remains unanswered: to what extent does the "recovery-through-competition" model create resilient cities? This paper challenges the perception that Rebuild has been an unassailable success through two methods. First, the competition's structure and three of its six winning proposals are critically assessed according to the Rebuild's core aims: innovation, feasibility, and resilience. Then, a broader critique of the recovery-through-competition model is developed around the process, politics, and products of Rebuild.

An Anatomy of Rebuild by Design
Rebuild launched in the summer of 2013 as a four-stage, interdisciplinary design competition to "promote innovation

BIG Team, "Battery Berm and Bridging Berm."

by developing regionally-scalable but locally-contextual solutions that increase resilience in the region."[10] The first stage, an RFP, generated 148 team submissions, from which 10 were chosen to proceed. The second stage provided each team with a unique site to research and the third challenged those teams to develop design proposals for their respective sites.[11] The competition concluded in June 2014 with the selection of six winning proposals by a national jury of design and planning experts. In the fourth stage, these six proposals received a share of approximately $1 billion in federal recovery funding to further refine and, in some cases, construct an initial phase of the project. Three of the teams focused on sites in New York City: the Bjarke Ingels Group (BIG), PennDesign and Olin (Penn/Olin), and SCAPE. Their sites vary widely, but their collective attention on the breadth of issues threatening New York's coastline provides an intriguing framework for assessing Rebuild.[12] The BIG proposal develops an infrastructural strategy for armoring Manhattan's Financial District, while the Penn/Olin and SCAPE proposals blend physical infrastructure, social policy, and economic development into a pair of resilience strategies in Hunts Point and Staten Island, respectively. But the unifying factor between these proposals rests in their shared socio-political context and in their limited scale. Put another way, each of these proposals focuses on a densely settled coastal community within New York that is geographically delimited. The winning proposals excluded from this assessment included a comprehensive plan for Hoboken, New Jersey, a restoration and management plan for the Meadowlands, New Jersey, and a regional plan for Long Island, New York.

BIG and the "BIG U" for Southern Manhattan

The BIG U proposal for Southern Manhattan is comprised of three components: (1) the Battery Berm, (2) the Bridging Berm, and (3) a retractable flood barrier along strategic portions of FDR Drive. Each berm anchors a sweeping network of green infrastructure aimed at integrating recreation and flood protection around the borough's Financial District and Lower East Side. The retractable barriers along FDR Drive provide ephemeral flood control between the berms. Together, the three elements form a U-shaped system of flood protection around Southern Manhattan, completely reshaping the borough's iconic waterfront in the process. This approach appears to build on the "New Urban Ground" proposal developed by dlandstudio for the 2010 *Rising Currents* exhibition at MoMA.[13]

BIG's proposal received $335 million, the highest amount awarded to a Rebuild finalist.[14] But the project's wholesale reconfiguration of Southern Manhattan's waterfront raises some important concerns about the proposal and Rebuild in general. At an estimated cost of $1.2 billion for phase one, implementing all or most of the proposal would be a multi-

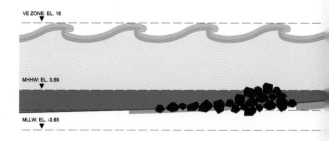

billion dollar,[15] decades-long endeavor.[16] This is problematic for at least three reasons. First, Rebuild failed to identify a long-term funding or financing strategy for delivering its winning proposals. The more time that passes, the less likely the city or the federal government is to prioritize funding for the BIG U. Second, the competition's novelty rests in its decision to assign a different site to each team. This leaves New Yorkers without a true point of reference with which to assess the merits of BIG's proposal. Though this a competition-wide issue, it is especially troublesome for this proposal given its specific site and high cost. Finally, the competition's approach to public engagement rests dangerously close to what Arnstein describes as "tokenism" or "non-participation."[17] Public meetings appeared sparsely attended and often served as a mechanism for communicating information to residents rather than engaging in dialogue with them. But the uncertainty surrounding the BIG U's timeline could actually provide BIG and HUD with the time necessary to step back from their vision and truly engage with New Yorkers on the future of this site.

Penn/Olin's "Lifelines" for Hunts Point (The Bronx)

The Penn/Olin proposal for Hunts Point contains four overlapping elements: [1] The Flood Protection Levee Lab, [2] the Livelihoods initiative, [3] the Maritime Emergency Supply Line Hub, and [4] the "Cleanways" tri-generation refrigeration facility.[18] The Lab and Livelihoods initiatives

1 "NYC Hazards: NYC Hurricane History," The Official Website of the City of New York, accessed July 30, 2014, http://www. nyc.gov/html/oem/html/hazards/storms_ hurricanehistory.shtml. This includes discussion of Hurricane Irene, a tropical storm that made landfall in August 2011. Irene was initially predicted to directly impact New York City, initiating the mass-evacuation of 375,000 residents and the citywide mobilization of first responders. However, the storm shifted shortly before making landfall, sparing the city all but isolated and minor incidences of flooding and wind damage. This likely contributed to the city's poor preparation as Superstorm Sandy approached New York.

2 John Englander, *High Tide on Main Street: Rising Sea Level and the Coming Coastal Crisis* (Boca Raton, FL: The Science Bookshelf, 2012).

3 Eugenie Birch & Susan Wachter, *Rebuilding Urban Places after Disaster: Lessons from Hurricane Katrina* (Philadelphia: University of Pennsylvania Press, 2006). Hurricane Katrina caused at least $108 billion in property damage, killed 1,833 people, displaced hundreds of thousands of New Orleans residents, and is considered the most destructive natural disaster in American history.

4 Chris Reed & Nina-Marie Lister, *Projective Ecologies* (Cambridge, MA: Actar, 2014).

5 Robert Olshansky & Laurie Johnson, *Clear as Mud: Planning for the Rebuilding of New Orleans* (Chicago: APA Planners Press, 2010).

6 "Hurricane Sandy Rebuilding Strategy: Stronger Communities, A Resilient Region,"

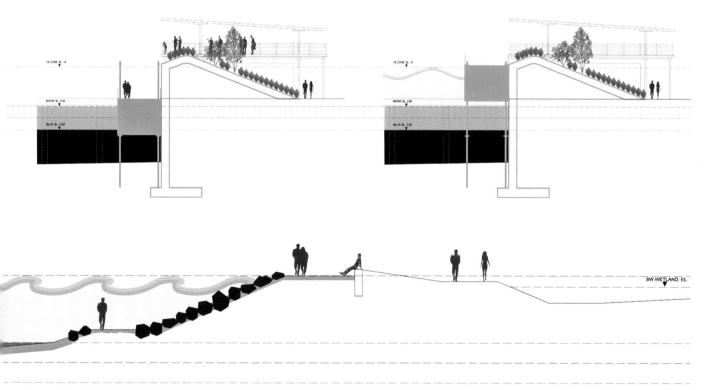

Penn/Olin, "Passive floodgate system and seawall variations."

Penn/Olin, "Conceptual Plan."

deliver a mutually reinforcing blend of design and policy innovation. The Lab merges conventional flood control with applied research space for testing experimental materials, designed ecologies, and new management protocols. Its dual purpose as a space for protection and innovation epitomizes a core principle of resilience theory: to facilitate adaptation amidst uncertainty by learning from past experience.[19] The Livelihoods initiative is a policy mechanism aimed at preserving a significant share of the Lab's permanent jobs for local residents. This would bolster the skills and earning power of the community's local workforce. Lifelines also calls for the creation of a Maritime Emergency Supply Lines Hub—an ephemeral logistics base capable of leading emergency relief efforts during future flood events—along the shoreline. The final component, Cleanways, centers on the construction of a tri-generation refrigeration warehouse within the Hunts Point food distribution center.[20] The Lifelines proposal received $20 million from HUD.[21]

Lifelines' blend of physical infrastructure, social policy, and economic development clearly delivers on the competition's core goals. But its use of social policy also raises three unique issues for the project. First, the Levee Lab creates organizational tensions, as it remains unclear who would manage the conventional flood-control system, who might direct the research, and how they would interact. Second, the proposal's workforce development recommendations may encounter resistance from local unions. Assessing how these unions might respond to the proposal is difficult given the paucity of information regarding public meetings available from Rebuild. Third, the competition's insistence on producing designs that are contextually sensitive yet scalable across the region may prove unrealistic. The Penn/Olin proposal focuses acutely on Hunts Point and none of its four elements appear well suited to regional extrapolation. Held to this standard, Lifelines (and most, if not all, of the winning proposals) may be perceived as a failure. But if its products prove non-exportable, perhaps the proposal's integrative methods can deliver on Rebuild's call for projects of regional significance.

SCAPE and "Living Breakwaters" around Staten Island

The SCAPE proposal for Staten Island is organized around a series of oyster reefs and other designed ecologies. The reefs—first proposed in Kate Orff's "Oyster-tecture" project within the 2010 *Rising Currents* exhibition at the MoMA—are seductive in their simplicity.[22] The Living Breakwaters act to reduce wave energy and improve local water quality, in addition to providing opportunities for local economic development through aquaculture and eco-tourism. Also, the concept's modularity enables SCAPE to employ a successive series of pilot projects and, in doing so, to calibrate the Living Breakwaters iteratively as it proceeds

The Hurricane Sandy Rebuilding Task Force, accessed July 30, 2014, http://portal.hud.gov/hudportal/documents/huddoc?id=hsrebuildingstrategy.pdf.

7 "A Stronger, More Resilient New York," The City of New York's Special Initiative for Rebuilding and Resilience, accessed July 30, 2014, available at http://www.nyc.gov/html/sirr/downloads/pdf/final_report/Ch_13_CriticalNetwork_Final_singles.pdf. Shortly after the report's publication, New York elected Bill De Blasio to succeed Michael Bloomberg as mayor. It is unclear how closely he plans to follow the report's recommendations.

8 "Executive Order – Establishing the Hurricane Sandy Rebuilding Task Force," The White House Office of the Press Secretary, accessed July 29, 2014, http://www.whitehouse.gove/the-press-office/2012/12/07/executive-order-establishing-hurricane-sandy-rebuilding-tas-force. The Hurricane Sandy Rebuilding Task Force, authorized by President Obama through Executive Order 13632, is an inter-agency collaboration charged with leading the federal government's recovery efforts throughout the Northeast.

9 "Fact Sheet: National Disaster Resilience Competition," The White House Office of the Press Secretary, accessed August 10, 2014, http://www.whitehouse.gov/the-press-office/2014/06/14/fact-sheet-national-disaster-resilience-competition. This competition is being funded with approximately $1 billion of federal aid initially appropriated for the post-Sandy recovery throughout the Northeast.

10 "Promoting Resilience Post-Sandy through Innovative Planning and Design," U.S. Department of Housing and Urban Development: Rebuild by Design, accessed July 10, 2014, http://portal.hud.gov/hudportal/documents/huddoc?id=REBUILDBYDESIGNBRIEF.pdf.

11 Ibid.

12 "Finalists," Rebuild by Design, accessed July 10, 2014, available at http://www.rebuildbydesign.org/winners-and-finalists/.

13 See Barry Bergdoll, *Rising Currents: Projects for New York's Waterfront* (New York: The Museum of Modern Art, 2011).

14 Graham Beck, "Massive New Storm-Protection Barrier Funded for Lower Manhattan," *Next City*, June 2, 2014, accessed July 15, 2014, http://www.nextcity.org/daily/entry/massive-new-storm-protection-barrier-funded-for-lower-manhattan/.

15 Inae Oh, "Could this 'BIG U' Save NYC from Another Superstorm Sandy?" *The Huffington Post*, June 3, 2014, accessed July 15, 2014, http://www.huffingtonpost.com/2014/06/03/rebuild-by-design-_n_5438603.html/.

16 Klaus Jacob, "Climate Scientist: Manhattan Will Need Venice-Like Canals to Stop Flooding," *Next City*, June 25, 2014, accessed July 30, 2014, http://www.nextcity.org/daily/entry/climate-scientist-manhattan-needs-venice-like-canals-flooding/.

17 Sherry Arnstein, "A Ladder of Citizen Participation," *Journal of the American Institute of Planners* 35 (1969): 216-224.

18 Hunts Point is a working-class community in The Bronx and is home to the New York Region's primary food distribution center. Every

towards full implementation. The project's ecological infrastructure is bolstered through a series of "water hubs" along the shoreline, which act as social anchors for neighborhoods along the waterfront by providing opportunities for recreation, public space, and educational programming. Living Breakwaters received $60 million in funding from HUD.[23]

The modularity and redundancy created by the proposal hews closely to the central tenets of resilience theory, and its creative use of oysters as an organizing device clearly fulfills the competition's desire for innovation.[24] But the project's reliance upon crustaceans creates a troubling vulnerability to an incipient threat from climate change: ocean acidification. Oyster farms throughout the Pacific Northwest are already facing species collapse as a result of rising ocean acidity.[25] Would the Living Breakwaters proposal be possible in a future scenario that limited or foreclosed upon the viability of oysters around Staten Island?[26] Also, despite SCAPE's use of hydrological modeling to test the efficacy of their proposal under existing conditions, it is not clear how the reefs would perform as sea levels continue to rise. But the project's modularity and deliberate phasing does provide for ample time and opportunity to address these concerns.

Can We Rebuild by Design?

As the Rebuild competition drew to a close, HUD announced its policy successor: the "National Disaster Resilience Competition."[27] HUD's decision to extrapolate the post-Sandy model of recovery-through-competition is unsurprising given the competition's fawning press coverage, the massive investment of financial and political capital by HUD and its partner organizations, and the resulting perception that Rebuild has been an unequivocal success.[28] But rushing to launch a national-scale competition before Rebuild has been independently assessed is a risky proposition.

The development of more critical perspectives on Rebuild is vital in determining whether it is a model worth replicating. Scholars exploring the competition's *processes* should consider three important lines of inquiry: (1) to what extent is the recovery-through-competition model producing projects of similar or higher quality than traditional means of urban design and development?; (2) to what extent is the model's emphasis on expediency foreclosing on meaningful levels of dialogue with local communities?; and (3) to what extent has the experience of the design firms been

SCAPE, "Living Breakwaters."

perishable food item available to the region's 22 million residents passes through this center.

19 Andrew Zolli & Ann Marie Healy, *Resilience: Why Things Bounce Back* (New York: Free Press, 2012).

20 "A Stronger, More Resilient New York," The City of New York's Special Initiative for Rebuilding and Resilience.

21 "Finalists," Rebuild by Design.

22 Barry Bergdoll and Michael Oppenheimer, *Rising Currents: Projects for New York's Waterfront* (New York: The Museum of Modern Art, 2011).

23 "Finalists," Rebuild by Design.

24 Zolli & Healy, *Resilience: Why Things Bounce Back*, 61–90.

25 Richard Feely et al., "Scientific Summary of Ocean Acidification in Washington State Marine Waters: Washington Shellfish Initiative Blue Ribbon Panel," *NOAA Special Report*, accessed August 10, 2014, https://fortress.wa.gov/ecy/publications/publications/1201016.pdf/.

26 Nina Bednarsek et al., "Extensive Dissolution of Live Pteropods in the Southern Ocean," *Nature Geoscience* 5 (2012): 881–885.

27 Will Doig, "HUD Announces $1 Billion Competition for Disaster Recovery Ideas," *Next City*, July 16, 2014, accessed August 10, 2014, http://www.nextcity.org/daily/entry/hud-announces-1-billion-competition-for-new-disaster-recovery-ideas.

28 Graham Beck, "Building for Resilience without the Feds Breathing Down Your Neck," *Next City*, March 6, 2014, accessed July 30, 2014, http://www.nextcity.org/daily/entry/building-for-resilience-without-the-feds-breathing-down-your-neck.

29 Kevin Fox Gotham & Miriam Greenberg, *Crisis Cities: Disaster and Redevelopment in New York and New Orleans* (Oxford: Oxford University Press, 2014).

positive or negative, and how might that experience influence the replicability of Rebuild in other contexts? The salience of these inquiries rests in the novelty of Rebuild, which eschewed the traditional design competition model by assigning different sites to each team. This provides an opportunity to assess both the internal products of Rebuild as well as a more comparative exploration of the conventional and recovery-through-competition models of post-disaster design. Meanwhile, scholars interested in the *products* of Rebuild should consider at least three additional fields of inquiry: (1) how should the performance of these resilience-oriented projects be evaluated and to what end?; (2) to what extent did each team's assigned site influence the jury's decision to select the winning proposals?; and (3) to what extent are these projects and their diversion of Community Development Block Grants[29] from traditional anti-poverty measures affecting spatial inequality?

Rebuild provides a robust collection of ideas and information for designers, policy-makers, and scholars to adopt, adapt, and assess. But if the competition's success aims to move beyond rhetoric and towards reality, these six lines of inquiry should be addressed. Only then might a national model premised on the idea of recovery-through-competition adhere to the core principle of the very resilience it aims to create: the ability to learn from the past in order to adapt to and prepare for the future.

CLAIRE HOCH
BOOK REVIEW: PROJECTIVE ECOLOGIES

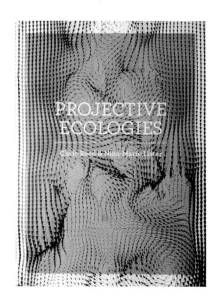

Claire Hoch is a designer with McGregor Coxall in Melbourne, Australia. She holds a Masters of Landscape Architecture from the University of Pennsylvania and a Bachelors of Fine Art and Critical Theory from Carnegie Mellon University.

╋ DESIGN, ECOLOGY, REPRESENTATION

Chris Reed and Nina Marie Lister (eds), *Projective Ecologies* (New York: Actar and Harvard GSD, 2014), 288 pages, Hardcover, RRP $34.95.

Edited by Chris Reed and Nina-Marie Lister, *Projective Ecologies* is a collection of new and reprinted essays concerned with the merging subjects of ecology, design, and urbanism. The publication ensues from the 2010 symposium "Critical Ecologies" at the Harvard GSD Department of Landscape Architecture. In addition to some papers from the symposium, Reed and Lister include a selection of foundational texts from the science of ecology, coupled with a collection of images from speculative design projects by landscape architects. By bringing together science and art in this way, the book tracks the absorption of ideas on complex adaptive systems into contemporary design discourse. The book's aim appears to be the establishment of a canonical collection of essays and images as the key terms of reference for how we now describe and design a world that is, according to the editors, "increasingly recognized as a hybrid of culture and nature, where old dualisms are being supplanted by transdisciplinary thinking, uneasy synergies, complex networks, and surprising collaborations."[1]

The introductory essay by Reed and Lister, "Parallel Genealogies", traces the progression of contemporary theories of ecology through three broadly defined lineages: the natural sciences, the humanities, and design (landscape architecture). The story is well known: a reorientation from modernist notions of order, stability and determinism toward models of indeterminacy and, more recently, resilience. While aiming to illuminate the growing alignment between ecology and design thinking in recent years, the editors are critical of practitioners' lagging engagement with complexity, adaptation and interdisciplinary approaches. With a small section in the introduction devoted to ecological design practices from the work of Ian McHarg and others into the early 2000s, "design thinking" in this collection is generally limited to academic discourse, not professional landscape practice and works. Reed and Lister's stated goal is to inspire a new generation of designers to develop methodologies aligned with and emerging from what they present as ecological models spanning the past few decades.

The contributions are organized into four sections: Emergent Ideas, Ecological Thinking; Anthro-Ecologies, Hybridity; Ecology, Cities, and Design; and Paths Forward. Classics such as James Corner's "Ecology and Landscape as Agents of Creativity" will be well known to readers, but others less so. For example, Christopher Hight's essay "Designing Ecologies" offers an overview of the philosophical underpinnings to the book's themes, questioning the acceptance of ecology into design channeled through the widespread use of the term sustainability and at the same time critiquing the design disciplines' distrust of "objective" science. Hight's argument for a "projective ecology" rejects modernist binaries and endorses Landscape Urbanism's push for design as both an expression of and catalyst for change in dynamic systems. The following three reprinted texts by C.S. Holling and M.A. Goldberg, Richard T.T. Forman et al., and Daniel Botkin ground this treatise, providing a socio-scientific foundation for the implications of contemporary ecological theory on design and planning.

Erle Ellis's essay "Anthropogenic Taxonomies" describes his recent work in developing a novel mapping method of anthromes, a reconception of the ecological land classification system of biomes that defines geographic regions based on contiguous climatic conditions that, without human intervention, provide a basis for ecological communities. His recognition of novel ecosystems (those permanently reshaped by human interaction) is prescient in the face of the global impact of climate change. Similarly, in "The Flora of the Future", Peter Del Tredici embraces novel ecosystems as not only valuable but essential contributions to the urban experience. The essay re-articulates his 2010 book *Wild Urban Plants* in which he argues for the acceptance of what are generally referred to as 'weeds' into the lexicon of landscape architects.

Robert Cook's 1999 essay "Do Landscapes Learn?" outlines the evolution of ecological theory in the 20th century and speculates on a landscape architecture that is based on a true understanding of ecological science and a practice that is embedded in temporality. As he explains, "For an ecologist, what is interesting about nature is what happened yesterday and how it informs us about what might happen tomorrow. The temporality of nature *is* nature, and insights based on spatial perceptions alone are highly suspect without an understanding of the underlying dynamic processes that created the spatial configuration."[2] His argument extends to a critique of a purely metaphorical or aesthetic understanding of ecosystem dynamics, one that dominated certain academic circles in reaction to McHarg's positivist approach to ecological planning.

Nestled between each chapter is a series of curated drawings organized by five themes: Dynamics, Succession, Emergence, Resilience, and Adaptability. Each section is introduced by a sentence or two from the editors: where Lister's introductions tend toward an explanation of the theme, Reed's are more abstract and metaphorical, interpreting the phenomena in design terms. The visual narratives that follow attempt to show how designers have appropriated and interpreted the language of ecology and as such reveals both the power of representation and its pitfalls. And here is the interesting problem the book–intentionally or not–circumscribes: ecological science has changed the way late 20th-century and early 21st-century landscape architecture is conceived of and practiced, but those conceptions and practices may indeed be misinterpretations of the science. In short, the designers' imaging of complex scientific ideas makes ecology look somehow easy or certain, almost invariably beautiful and ultimately manageable. Problematically, the editors never explain the rationale for their particular selections, nor do they engage critically with the images.

Interestingly, very few of these images have manifested in material practice. For example, the drawings categorized as 'process' are not in fact part of real processes, rather they are process-depicted: diagrams of fluctuating systems replete with overly zealous arrows. These contextless drawings appear pseudo-scientific and achieve a level of visual complexity, but their pretenses to generating real processes of ecological change are questionable. Why not include working drawings or adaptive iterations of real projects? This might help us see ecological thinking through the medium of design, rather than only through the refined illustrative diagram and the written word. But that would be a different book, a messier book!

Ambitious in scope and optimistic in tone, this volume presents some classic texts on landscape ecology and planning that have inspired contemporary designers along with writing by inspired designers on the importance of reimagining the role of ecology in design practice. The editors aimed to present a multiplicity of research in parallel fields and to speculate on new paths forward for design. But the book remains primarily internal and discursive, missing the opportunity to include less-known texts from other disciplines and dismissing contemporary design practice's engagement with ecological process as nascent. Besides a brief discussion of pre-2000s process-oriented design in the editors' essay, there is no mention of any built projects or design studios actively engaging these ideas. This is a shame because the two editors have their feet in both practice and academia, giving them a prime opportunity to reconcile some of the discrepancies between the two. Design is powerful as a discipline because at its foundation it is a material practice that has immense immaterial implications. But if this book has now achieved a sense of canonical foundation and formalized the coming together of the science of ecology and design, then it also underscores the need for the next symposium and book to be more about material practice.

1 Chris Reed & Nina-Marie Lister, "Ecological Thinking, Design Practices," in *Projective Ecologies*, eds Chris Reed & Nina-Marie Lister (New York: Actar, 2014), 17.

2 Robert Cook, "Do Landscapes Learn? Ecology's New Paradigm and Design in Landscape Architecture," in *Projective Ecologies*, ibid. Originally published in Michael Conan, ed., *Environmentalism in Landscape Architecture* (Washington DC: Dumbarton Oaks, 2000).

IN CONVERSATION WITH
RICHARD T. T. FORMAN

+ LANDSCAPE ECOLOGY, URBAN PLANNING,
  URBAN ECOLOGY

Richard T.T. Forman is a renowned ecologist who pioneered the increasingly important field of landscape ecology. Also considered the 'father' of road ecology, Forman has devoted much of his distinguished career to cataloguing, measuring, and improving the ecological performance of different settlement patterns at a landscape scale. A key characteristic of his career has been his ability to move between the sciences and the arts. Forman received his PhD from the University of Pennsylvania and is now a Research Professor at Harvard University where he teaches ecological principles in the Graduate School of Design. His latest book is *Urban Ecology: Science of Cities*.

+ Your book *Urban Ecology: Science of Cities* is almost a manual for how landscape architects, architects, planners and other experts can apply ecology to urban environments. Do you think designers get it?

After 30 years' working in this stimulating milieu, I think the jury is still out. It's still unclear to me that designers and planners as a whole have grasped the importance of a solid foundation in water, wildlife, biodiversity, soil, microclimate, fish movement, and so forth. I salute the exceptions as real leaders. Note that this book spells out the array of urban ecology principles, but largely leaves their application for society to the creative professionals.

+ Where are our shortcomings, do you think?

Academically and professionally in studios, projects, and plans, the mega-opportunity staring at us is an insistence by faculty or the lead designer to consider plants, animals, air, water, and soil as both a primary foundation and often a key solution. Think of Olmsted in the 19th century on the edge of Boston designing for transportation, sewage, flooding, vegetation, and aesthetics. He did it so well that the Emerald Necklace is still important within Boston today. But what happened after Olmsted I never understood. Sometime in the 20th century, most planners and designers largely tossed natural systems aside, instead focusing on socio-economics and public policy. Imagine these creative professionals now raising and leveraging their knowledge of natural systems to increasingly provide the core solutions for society's current global issues.

+ How have your methods of representation changed over time to model and represent increasingly complex issues?

I would like to say that they haven't changed. My feeling is that simple models are an advantage. I especially like simple spatial models, say, with only one or two main variables. Increasing the variables increases complexity, and studies have shown that very few human minds can envision four variables co-varying. If we want our ideas or plans implemented, we must get through to decision-makers, the mayor, the government, whomever. A decision-maker must do three things with your plan or model. First, he or she has to understand it; if three or four main variables are present, the client may simply trust you and say 'fine'. But second, the decision-maker has to explain the design to the public, as well as to staff. Third, and toughest, she or he has to defend the model against critics. Complex models or plans may not reach the third step and your idea goes nowhere. The best ideas and models may be complex, but for implementation they are simple and normally spatial. Spatial provides a common base and lingo, and is the way I think. We can communicate effectively around a map or satellite image with the CEO and mayor, but also with geographers, social scientists, and engineers. The key is both the quality of an idea and how well it is expressed. National Geographic's history has taught us that images alone are usually inadequate but text alone is also inadequate. Good visual/spatial combined with good text is most compelling. Let me add an insight that Joan Nassauer, a landscape architect at the University of Michigan, taught me. For an article I wrote several years ago, she pointed out that if I want a plan implemented, it better be visually attractive. Otherwise it will not engage the public. That's a simple, really important guideline that I, as a scientist, would not have highlighted.

+ You describe a spatial model as something that imparts tools to a designer to act on a site anywhere in the world. Can you speak to the relevance of site-specificity in terms of cultural sensitivities and spatial sensitivities?

I teach principles. These are different from case studies and site-specificity. Principles will work anywhere in the world, and the search for principles is also my thought process. I look for relative universality, meaning that an idea or pattern is important, widely applicable, and relatively independent of geography and land use. Such principles are the really exciting models that work in different countries and with different cultures.

On the other hand, there are some advantages of site specificity in that you get closer to the specific species present and what people cue in to. Most people care about special small places, like their house plot, a pond, or a neighborhood. They care less about larger areas – an urban region and especially global issues. Caring *about* a place leads to caring *for* it. Think globally, plan regionally, then act locally.

+ Cities seem to be impinging more and more on surrounding landscapes – do you think that there is any true wilderness left?

There is certainly wilderness, but it is far away, like large tracts of Canada, Siberia, Brazil. In most of the world, agriculture surrounds the city. In North America, we have started sprawling out beyond the rural agricultural zone into semi-natural areas. Such nearby surrounding areas are not wilderness, as they conspicuously reflect decades or centuries of often-diverse human use. Where cities bump into semi-natural areas we may see the greatest land degradation and change – yet change represents opportunity for designers and planners. I say to my students that generally you can have a small positive impact in a city center, but if you want to have a big impact, go out into this dynamic urban edge where solutions really matter for both nature and people. Antoni Gaudi designed the magical Parque Guell out on the edge of Barcelona, and Frederick Olmsted's Emerald Necklace was created on the dynamic edge of Boston.

+ Let's talk a little about your design students. How have they benefited from collaboration with the sciences?

One reason I began working with designers and planners is because, almost always, good design requires a good understanding of ecological systems. Some students embrace this idea seriously and some still consider it tangential. The percentage of students who grasp the central importance of natural systems is increasing, but alas slowly. I have some optimism. Yet after 50 years of environmentalism as one of the major ideas of history, it is surprising how few professionals recognize and use ecology effectively for society.

When a president or mayor creates a blue-ribbon panel for a big land-use issue, a planner or designer should be on the panel. I'd like to see my former students on leadership panels of the future. Jumpstarting the students with some solid scientific literacy now will greatly enhance their effectiveness in working with engineers, economists, soil scientists, and others for sustainable solutions.

+ So that is really the missing link in terms of our agency of design?

Yes, ecology or natural systems is the missing link. One could say that economics is, but I don't think so. Going back to that dynamic perimeter zone of a city, landscape ecologists and conservation biologists are increasingly getting projects and plans there that ecology-savvy planners and designers should have. I was hired to do a project/plan for the Region of Barcelona, a world-class city with a long history of brilliant planning and design by famous people. Why did the mayor and chief architect invite me for this? Probably because I was an ecological scientist, was spatially oriented, and respected, and could communicate well with planners, architects, and biologists. In view of UN population statistics, big problems needing solutions lurk just outside the city. Who will make history by stepping forward to lead with appropriate designs and plans?

+ Do you believe that the efficiency and sustainability of a design lies in interpreting organic patterns often found in nature?

If we just create rectilinear patterns for society, we'll simply continue to pour money into maintaining and repairing them. That design is expensive, ineffective, and unsustainable. Imagine maintaining a rectilinear grid system with buildings where you largely ignore the powerful flows of water, air, animals, soil, geology, and so on. The ubiquitous patterns of nature are quite different – irregular, fine-textured, aggregated, fractal, dissimilar in size, heterogeneous in type, moving, flowing, changing over time, and at many spatial and temporal scales. Extensive wild areas, which I relish and often spend time in, are essential for biological conservation. In contrast, an urban rectilinear pattern does provide human efficiencies–for measurement, construction, movement–but if a pattern requires constant maintenance and repair, it's not a very good design. That's why it is important to identify the major horizontal flows and movements across the land, such as groundwater, floodwater, meandering streams, wildlife movements, streamline airflows, vehicle traffic, and walkers. Concurrently we should pinpoint areas in the surroundings likely to markedly change. After mapping these important flows and changes, then arrange the objects: roads, buildings, wetlands, parks, sewage treatment facility...whatever the challenge. For any plan or project, first map the flows and change sites; then arrange objects.

+ Your career has been defined by an interest in broad-scale ecological patterns, but your last book concerns urban ecology – why this late turn toward the city?

Why, that was quite logical. After numerous published articles and four books on landscape ecology, one road ecology book, and two on urban regions, burrowing into the ecology of cities and suburbs was the obvious next frontier. Also, for 30 years landscape architects, planners, and many other professionals have challenged me with urban ecology queries, which I too often deferred.

But wait! Suppose 150 years ago, ecology had begun in cities instead of in forest, pond and farmland. Numerous features are fundamentally different in urban and natural lands. Most urban ecology research has tried to apply theories, models and concepts from natural land to the city. That's really awkward. Rather, we should be developing distinctive urban ecology principles around the distinctive characteristics of built areas. It's exciting to ponder principles linking organisms, built structures, and the physical environment where people are concentrated. Future ecology texts should become 25% urban ecology. More students will see their future career in urban ecology. Indeed they will be especially interested in what landscape designers, planners and others are doing. Catalyzing the urban ecology frontier with this relatively comprehensive book should draw the fields closer together. In short, I see a great opportunity to begin together creating wonderful cities and suburbs, for both nature and us.

Opposite: "Patches, Edges and Boundaries", from Richard T.T. Forman, Wenche E. Dramstad & James D. Olson, *Landscape Ecology Principles in Landscape Architecture and Land-Use Planning* (1996).

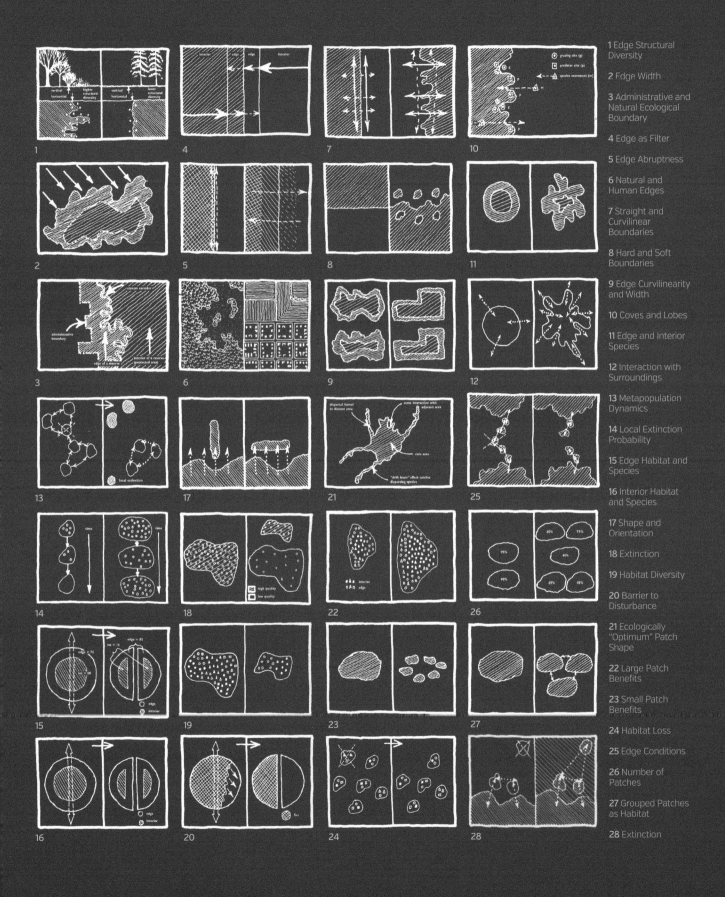

1 Edge Structural Diversity

2 Edge Width

3 Administrative and Natural Ecological Boundary

4 Edge as Filter

5 Edge Abruptness

6 Natural and Human Edges

7 Straight and Curvilinear Boundaries

8 Hard and Soft Boundaries

9 Edge Curvilinearity and Width

10 Coves and Lobes

11 Edge and Interior Species

12 Interaction with Surroundings

13 Metapopulation Dynamics

14 Local Extinction Probability

15 Edge Habitat and Species

16 Interior Habitat and Species

17 Shape and Orientation

18 Extinction

19 Habitat Diversity

20 Barrier to Disturbance

21 Ecologically "Optimum" Patch Shape

22 Large Patch Benefits

23 Small Patch Benefits

24 Habitat Loss

25 Edge Conditions

26 Number of Patches

27 Grouped Patches as Habitat

28 Extinction

IMAGE CREDITS

WILD SPRING 2015

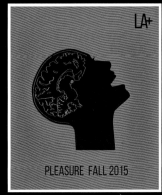

PLEASURE FALL 2015

TYRANNY SPRING 2016

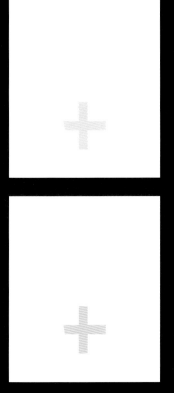

LA+
INTERDISCIPLINARY JOURNAL
OF LANDSCAPE ARCHITECTURE

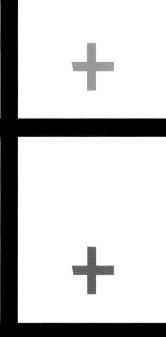

UPCOMING ISSUES

LA+ (Landscape Architecture Plus) from the University of Pennsylvania School of Design is the first truly interdisciplinary journal of landscape architecture. Within its pages you will hear not only from designers, but also from historians, artists, philosophers, psychologists, geographers, sociologists, planners, scientists, and others. Our aim is to reveal connections and build collaborations between landscape architecture and other disciplines by exploring each issue's theme from multiple perspectives.

LA+ brings you a rich collection of contemporary thinkers and designers in two issues each year. To subscribe follow the links at WWW.LAPLUSJOURNAL.COM.